Leading
School
Improvement

A Framework for Action

Leading *School* Improvement

A Framework for Action

JOSEPH MURPHY

LearningSciencesInternational

LEARNING AND PERFORMANCE MANAGEMENT

1400 Centrepark Blvd, Suite 1000
West Palm Beach, FL 33401
717-845-6300

email: pub@learningsciences.com
learningsciences.com

Printed in the United States of America
20 19 18 17 16 15   2 3 4

Publisher's Cataloging-in-Publication Data
Murphy, Joseph.
  Leading school improvement / Joseph Murphy.
     pages cm
  ISBN: 978-1-941112-41-0 (pbk.)
1. Educational leadership. 2. Educational change. 3. School management and organization. I. Title.
  LB2805 .M816 2015
  371.2—dc23
                              [2015939537]

To all the EdD colleagues it has been my great privilege to teach.

Table of Contents

Acknowledgments

Learning Sciences International would like to thank the following reviewers:

John F. Ash
2014 Tennessee Middle School
  Principal of the Year
Central Magnet School
Murfreesboro, Tennessee

Guy Banicki
Assistant Professor
Illinois State University
Normal, Illinois

Ann Caine
Superintendent
Stillwater Public Schools
Stillwater, Oklahoma

Darren Guido
Supervisor of Instruction
Capital School District
Dover, Delaware

Jared C. Wastler
2014 Maryland Assistant Principal
  of the Year
Liberty High School
Eldersburg, Maryland

About the Author

Joseph Murphy is the Frank W. Mayborn Chair of Education at Peabody College of Education at Vanderbilt University. He also has been a faculty member at the University of Illinois and The Ohio State University, where he was the William Ray Flesher Professor of Education.

In public schools, he has served as an administrator at the school, district, and state levels. His most recent appointment was as the founding president of the Ohio Principals Leadership Academy.

He is a past vice president of the American Educational Research Association (AERA) and an AERA Fellow.

Murphy directed the development of the Interstate School Leaders Licensure Consortium (ISLLC) Standards for School Leaders and chaired the research panel that produced the revisions to those standards. He led the team that developed the specifications with Educational Testing Service (ETS) for the School Leaders Licensure Assessment (SLLA). He is also one of the four cocreators of the Vanderbilt Assessment of Leadership in Education.

The Gift Giver

To unsettle and alloy that bewilderment with joy
To allow flight and provide an unseen scaffolding of support
To hold tightly while letting go

To correct with precision and warmth
To reveal mysteries and provide ladders for climbing to understanding

To challenge, to exhort, to demand
To push, to pull, to carry
To build, to empower
To respect and acknowledge, to ennoble

To place one's own heart on the altar and one's own hands in the fire
To remember the forgotten

To feel, to share
To dance in celebration
To pass into the shadows

To teach

Introduction

Most of my career has been spent working on the broad topic of school improvement and the place of school leaders in that work. While much of those efforts have found their way into academic books and journal articles, some of the work has been directed to colleagues in leadership roles in schools and school districts. In this book, I pull fourteen of these practitioner-based articles into a cohesive narrative about leading school improvement. All of these pieces have been published over the past twenty years in outlets such as *Educational Leadership, Kappan,* and *Principal.* They appeared as I engaged with an ongoing series of research projects. For example, chapter 12, the newest piece, comes from my work on caring leadership over the last five years.

The purpose of this volume is to bring the articles together to explain the larger storyline of leading school improvement—to pull separate planets together into a universe with a gravitational pull of principals nurturing school success. I attempt to achieve this integration in two ways. First, I weave important ideas (e.g., leadership values) across the various chapters. Common threads such as "academic press" and "care" are thus integrated into the larger narrative. Second, I cluster the articles to provide rich narratives on three overlapping issues that define the book.

The opening part of the book includes five chapters that unpack the concept of pactice of leadership for principals, superintendents, and other school leaders. The focus here is less on the specific actions that leaders need to undertake than it is on the principles and values that define excellence in leadership in schools. Energy is devoted to helping school leaders understand that personal characteristics (e.g., persistence and passion) and virtues (e.g., courage and integrity) count more than behavioral descriptors. Our core argument is that absent these foundational touchstones, meaningful school leadership is impossible to reach. And if meaningful leadership is not sustainable, then neither is substantive school improvement work.

The second part of the book helps readers develop a much richer and deeper understanding of school improvement than is the norm in educational literature. The essential point is the understanding that the entire school improvement building rests on two essential pillars: academic press and supportive culture. Developing this wisdom and learning how to employ it in the quest for school improvement is considerably more valuable than mastering specific behavioral skills. So also are informed understandings of how social, political, and economic forces shape possibilities for school improvement. So too are deep understandings of what it means to lead in a community as opposed to a bureaucracy, a learning environment as opposed to a system of knowledge transmission, and a customer-oriented organization as opposed to a public monopoly.

The final part of the book goes further. No longer content to see the interplay within each of the concepts of leadership and school improvement, we weave these two constructs together into a unifying frame for promoting school success. In short, we attack the issue of leadership *for* school improvement. The work again allows the reader to go backstage in this production to see how leaders should work on the two core issues of ramping up academic press and fostering a productive culture, strategies that carry the reader beyond ideas disconnected from the "self" of leadership and the "DNA" of school improvement.

Part 1

Focusing the Lens on Leadership

Special Senses

Learning not to talk

Seeing beyond the surface

The power to listen, and hear

Seeing the wonder in the routine and ordinary

Hearing nonconfirming voices

Not overlooking opportunities to help

Chapter 1

The Five Intelligences of Leadership

Over the last century, practitioners and academics have looked at leadership with multiple lenses. They have directed the spotlight of understanding on various dimensions of leadership (e.g., transformational leadership, moral leadership). They have also carved leadership into numerous components, resulting in the creation of assorted taxonomies and frameworks. In this chapter, I bring another perspective on leadership to life—what is called the intelligences of leadership. My assessment is that five intelligences comprise the DNA of leadership: banked intelligence, fluid intelligence, connected intelligence, relational intelligence, and operational intelligence (see Figure 1.1). As you move through this chapter, I will discuss each concept in more detail.

Figure 1.1   The Five Intelligences of Leadership

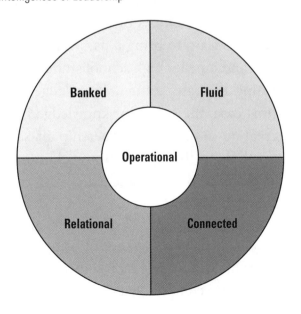

Banked Intelligence

Banked intelligence refers to the content knowledge essential to the task of leading—what academics refer to as crystallized intelligence. A good deal of banked intelligence is generic; it stretches across industries and positions. For example, we find here knowledge of strategies to resolve conflict effectively, successfully conduct a meeting, or craft a productive strategic plan. Other banked knowledge is industry specific, in this case educationally anchored. For example, we find here knowledge of the laws on student rights. There is also job-specific banked knowledge (e.g., that needed to be an athletic director or an assistant principal of student affairs). Finally, some banked knowledge is context specific (e.g., leading William Burnett Middle School in Fisher, Indiana, during the current school year). Knowledge of the teacher contract or the politics of the community could be essential at Burnett. Building content assets is always a wise idea; however, leaders need to be able to bring those assets to bear on specific challenges, opportunities, and problems, as I will discuss further in this chapter.

Fluid Intelligence

Fluid intelligence refers to the ability to think. That is, it is about the ability to puzzle through situations employing the banked knowledge at hand. The use of fluid intelligence is one of the essential ways that the need for new content knowledge is identified. Even more important, it is the main avenue through which oftentimes inert blocks of content are given meaning. For example, working through ways to bring a passively disengaged and lonely (or actively disengaged and hostile) high school student into the community will necessitate injecting life into content knowledge about pastoral care for adolescents. In this case, the subset of knowledge about student–adult relationships and creating authentic membership in school will need to be brought forth and thought through. Without fluid intelligence, banked knowledge can often sit in the vault untouched.

Connected Intelligence

Connected intelligence is the art and science of bringing pieces of the work narrative together in productive ways. In a number of venues over the years, I have argued that, given the complexity and turbulent world of schooling, growing alignment and coherence is a cardinal aspect of school leadership. Such is the work of connected intelligence. An example will be helpful here. There is abundant evidence that units (e.g., teachers, programs) and dimensions (e.g., budgets, goals) in schools often function as if they were in different galaxies. Working to craft all programs in a school around a particular point of view about student writing or a common perspective on student responsibility are illustrations of forging centers of gravity—that is, the use of connected intelligence.

Relational Intelligence

Relational intelligence maps onto dimensions of more generalized theories of intelligence. More specifically, it aligns with two aspects of Gardner's Theory of Multiple Intelligence: the intrapersonal and interpersonal domains. Relational intelligence means possessing and testing a robust understanding of self in social context (i.e., in the school community writ large). Relational intelligence honors the mirror of reflection—the wisdom to see oneself as he is as defined by self and others and the acknowledgment, understanding, and thoughtful examination of differences. In many ways, because this intelligence is profoundly personal and because many school leaders have learned the protective dysfunctionalities of denial, blame, withdrawal, and justification, this is an especially difficult intelligence to master and polish over time.

Relational intelligence is also about understanding others. It is the cocktail of dispositions, knowledge, and skills to work productively with people. We know that the great majority of principals' time is spent on interpersonal interactions. We also know historically that principals have failed most often when they lack relational intelligence. Understanding how to work in authentic ways with children, teachers and staff, and members of the extended community is difficult business. Even when it is in play, it is often pushed onto the margins by pressures to follow the thick binder of procedural guidance that directs schooling. Yet without relational intelligence, it is impossible for school leaders to succeed.

Operational Intelligence

The fifth domain of leadership is operational intelligence, also known as the ability to make things happen effectively in schools and school districts. It depends on the possession of the other intelligences. Surprisingly, and quite inappropriately, it is often dismissed as "management" or "technical skills." In reality, it is the knowledge to blend the various intelligences creatively and to positive effect in the face of work that needs doing and, of course, the ability to understand what work is required. It is often seen in anemic form in schools in cases where one or more of the other intelligences are underdeveloped. For example, we sometimes see principals operationalizing communities for teachers absent the relational intelligence required to make the work productive. In other cases, we see this work unfold without needed banked intelligence (i.e., the essential components of professional communities such as shared accountability and evidence-based collaborative work). On the other hand, operationalized intelligence emits a magical glow when it is in full bloom. Think of the elementary principal who has navigated the shoals of addressing student needs by changing the assignments of teacher colleagues mid-semester. Or the secondary school principal with the operational intelligence to successfully address a community crisis spawned by bullying in the school.

I acknowledge that there is an abundance of ways to think about leadership in general and school and district leadership in particular. I believe, however, that the intelligences of leadership provide a powerful framework to capture the work of school administrators. It opens new possibilities for thinking about the work. Even more important, it provides an especially robust architecture for the analysis of that work, helping leaders understand why certain actions worked and why others did not and pinpointing where intelligences need to be enhanced. It privileges learning, analysis, and action.

Chapter 2

Backstage Roles for School Leaders

Over the years, many colleagues have helped the profession conceptualize and portray school leadership. Much of this work has focused on important roles and functions that leaders perform to make schools operate effectively and move to higher levels of performance (e.g., evaluating instruction). I refer to this as "front stage" understandings and descriptions of school leadership. In this chapter, I move beyond this type of description to capture and portray a "backstage" understanding of leadership. All of my research over the last four decades leads to the conclusion that this backstage view is at least as important as more traditional perspectives—and often more significant. It allows leaders to peer into their roles in new ways, underscoring deeper and crosscutting understandings of their work, ones that carry a good deal of authenticity. Language matters a good deal and applying new lenses to leadership can, I maintain, be very productive. To begin, I separate this backstage work into three bundles: leaders as seedbed developers, glueing agents, and caregivers.

Seedbed Developers

The first law of school improvement is that structural changes do not predict school performance. Yet for almost the entire history of the profession of school administration, leaders have been and continue to be "importers" of structural interventions (e.g., block scheduling, looping, advisory periods). Many of these reforms are bought by schools. Others are gifts from district offices and states. There are two troublesome problems associated with this method of leadership. To begin with, structural changes (e.g., team teaching, cooperative learning) are often imported from venues without the goods (the

DNA) that made them effective in those places. The importing school leader often ends up with an empty box (e.g., an academy), one that lacks the power to accomplish what the structural design was brought forward to accomplish (e.g., trusting relationships between teachers and students). Equally critical, it is nearly impossible to get post-industrial structures to grow in the existing seedbeds of schools. For example, schools have a deep seedbed of learning built up from behaviorist understandings of teaching and learning. It is nearly impossible to get socially constructed reforms, such as authentic assessments or cooperative learning, to grow in a behaviorist seedbed. The soil is toxic. It will choke out these new perspectives on learning.

Thus, we see that it is productive to think of the role of principals as seedbed developers, not importers. This "backstage" perspective underscores the fact that the primary role of the principal is to rework the deeply entrenched seedbeds in the areas of teaching and learning, and school organization. Only then can important socially constructed and communal perspectives and ideas take root and flourish. Equally critical here, leaders need to help their schools come to understand and agree on the DNA or the core ideas they want to see grow in their schools before they worry about structural interventions. Structures can support DNA once a school knows what it wants, but structures rarely carry the DNA. This means that school leaders are seedbed developers, people who stay focused first and foremost on the right stuff, the DNA of improvement—not the boxes people incorrectly claim carry the DNA.

Glueing Agents

A second very powerful backstage way to highlight the essence of principal work is to describe these leaders as glueing agents. As an advance organizer, I note that this glueing work is about two activities: creating alignment, integration, and coherence and compressing variability. We start with an age-old reality about schools. That is, they are loosely linked places in which to work. On the leadership front, I am reminded of a great description I once heard in a speech by Larry Lezotte: Schools are places where individuals come to run their business (e.g., Mrs. Wall's fourth-grade class) surrounded by a common parking lot. Teachers have historically worked alone with little nonsymbolic interference from leaders. Understandings of learning and teaching have been fractured with teachers often following their own best ideas. At the school level, mission has had a weak pull on school activity. Resource allocations have been only loosely based on school goals.

Exceptional leaders are aggressive in resetting the dynamic of looseness. They search for domains that when aligned and cohered bring benefits to the array of actions in schools. Principals provide cohesion into schooling by inculcating core values into activities, or more accurately, scaffolding activities on essential values (e.g., making "care" the central dynamic of cocurricular activities). They infuse coordination into ideas such as leadership density and professional community. They ensure integration by glueing together quite loosely linked transitions in schools (e.g., from the elementary to middle school or the middle school to the high school). They weld back together the often tenuously connected worlds of teachers and administrators. They bolt together and give meaning to systems, policies, and practices that provide common direction and shared work. They are especially skillful in nurturing the growth of relational glue (i.e., trust) that allows coherence in schools to come to life.

Glueing work is also about compressing variability in schools. There is less inconsistency in schools shepherded by strong leaders. Effective leaders are essential to forging the parameters within which schooling unfolds. Work within these parameters tightens linkages and nurtures alignment. Work outside the parameters promotes loose couplings and undermines the integration essential for school and student success. I recall what another grandfather of effective schools, Ron Edmonds, often replied when asked about the essence of effective schools: It is all the people in the school acting in a consistent and aligned manner day in and day out across all aspects of the school.

Caregivers

Peeking backstage again, we see a third line of work that often goes unhighlighted on the front stage of school leadership, a mixture of concierge and homemaker. The core idea here is leader as *caregiver* (see chapter 12). This means that she is at the center of a good deal of action. Some of this comes with the role. But effective leaders are gifted at developing webs of care and support that are much denser than what is normal in schools. They provide a hub of knowledge about how things are and the best people with whom to connect to accomplish tasks. They offer advice to everyone. Not only do they turn up opportunities that are often unknown to teachers, but also they are advocates in securing access to those opportunities. In a related vein, effective leaders see themselves as caregivers to very extensive families of students, teachers, and extended stakeholders. Exceptional leaders understand that their job is as much about creating communities of care as it is about building academic press. They demonstrate the ability to make each person in the school feel known, valued, and respected. They work to ensure that everyone experiences meaningful affiliation and has ownership in the school. And they scaffold the role of caregiver on trusting relationships.

My argument is that there is more to school leadership than the front stage functions that are often highlighted in the literature on effective schools. It is not that these tasks are not essential. On the contrary, we would not have great schools if these functions were not attended to carefully. However, I believe that deeply embedded, crosscutting elements are equally important in telling the story of effective leaders. I refer to them as backstage functions—ones that while critical are often only dimly visible in the play unfolding on the front stage. In this chapter, I describe three of the most essential roles: seedbed developers, glueing agents, and caregivers.

Chapter 3

Three Layers of Leadership

A historical analysis of organizations reveals that few topics have received more attention than leadership. And when we spotlight the education industry specifically, we see that considerable space has been given over to the treatment of this concept. Academics, developers, and practitioners have all taken turns adding to our understanding of what school leadership is and how it unfolds in schools and districts. It is not my intention here to add to the realm of knowledge in this fashion. I do not offer another taxonomy of leadership. Such work is important; however, here I offer instead a parsimonious yet powerful frame for how to think about the leadership required to power school improvement. Specifically, I introduce the idea of "layers" of leadership. Based on my ongoing thirty-year analysis of the work of school leadership, I conclude that there are three such layers of work: acting from the heart, attending to the laws of school improvement, and practicing the craft of promoting academic press and community-anchored schooling.

The Bedrock: Acting From the Heart

A number of analysts over the years have labored to expose the essential bedrock or the foundational layer of "good" leadership, perhaps none more eloquently or effectively than Lee Bolman and Terry Deal in their cardinal volume, *Leading with Soul* (2011). While the idea is too mushy, too unscientific, and too far removed from behaviors to make many reviewers in today's environment comfortable, it is nearly impossible to find a highly effective school in which this bedrock is not fairly deep.

When you talk to principals about the essentials of their work (and when you examine cases of highly effective schools), you are almost never transported into a conversation that features a new curricular program or a new teacher evaluation system. The talk is of powerful advocacy for children and young people, about a very clear sense of priorities. You feel passion, commitment, and hope. You learn of the centrality of trusting relationships, of care and respect. You sense integrity and service.

This is the bedrock of great school leadership. In the rush toward scientific evidence and rationality, we ignore it at great peril. At the same time, it is essential but not sufficient. We do principals and superintendents no favor when we stop here or when we jump immediately to effective behaviors without helping leaders develop the required mid-layer of leadership, understanding the laws of school improvement.

The Scaffolding: Using the Principles of School Improvement

Effective leadership is more than the compilation of scores of "good" activities. If the ideas we discussed previously form the bedrock, then wisdom about the rules of school improvement is the architecture on which policies need to be written, systems and procedures need to be forged, and to which practices need to be connected. These rules give meaning to and shape the work of leadership in effective schools.

Good principals know the essential rules of how to build better schools; and they know that if they violate those rules, school improvement initiatives will die, no matter how much acclaim accompanies an intervention. They will die, either in a large and spectacular fashion or slowly by attrition. So what does this second essential layer of leadership look like? It is more wrought out work than is the bedrock material. It is more threaded and integrated. It is harder to see and feel. If the bedrock is a set of deep-seated and inherent principles, the scaffolding is a set of forged rules. For example, effective leaders understand that context always matters in improvement work. History is important. The level and type of school needs attention. All interventions need to be molded and shaped to fit the school. They also have learned that structures do not predict performance, that structures (e.g., block scheduling, detracking, academies) do not carry the seeds of success. The best principals do not make the often-committed and fatal assumption that bringing these new structures to school will automatically lead to success. The wisdom of practice has taught them that interventions need to be infused with meaning, so they work hard to make this happen.

In a similar fashion, they understand that in school improvement there is no silver bullet; improvement is always an array of integrated efforts. Effective leaders understand that bringing alignment and cohesion to change efforts is as important, or more important, than the individual actions themselves. They are aware that early trumps later and prevention trumps remediation. The use of these and the other overarching rules of school improvement makes up that second layer of effective leadership.

The Build Out: Creating Academic Press and a Community-Anchored Culture

Getting all youngsters to reach ambitious targets of academic and social success is complex and often difficult work. Leading from the heart and systematically applying the principles of school improvement set the stage to achieve that end. But leaders can be successful only if they add a third layer of actions. This layer is about a relentless attending to the two essential elements of great schools—academic press and a community-anchored learning environment. It is also about forging an alloy of the two, or wrapping them around each other like a coil of rope.

We know a good deal about the dimensions of this third layer of effective leadership. Academic press, for example, includes actions on a variety of fronts: ensuring that all children are confronted with and supported in reaching ambitious goals, engaging each youngster in a rigorous educational program, providing quality instruction that challenges students to move beyond their level of comfort, and so forth. Actions to bring forth a community-anchored school include creating a professional culture in which teachers share a sense of direction, work on practice in a collaborative manner, and hold each other accountable for student outcomes; ensuring that every child is known, cared for, and respected; and getting trusting relationships developed among teachers, between teachers and students, among students, and between educators in the school and parents.

We know a good deal about leadership. And we continue to learn more each day, to deepen the leadership narrative, and to craft a more nuanced story. At the same time, we spend insufficient time attending to how to "essentialize" this knowledge. What is the essence of effective leadership? How do we make sense of what we have learned? Ongoing work on my part convinces me that there are three layers of good leadership: acting from the heart; employing the rules of school improvement; and building up the two core elements of great schools, academic press and community-anchored organization. My research also leads me to conclude that leaders need to engage on all three fronts. Finally, I find that effective leadership is layered, with principles and rules required for layer-three actions to take root.

Chapter 4

The Four Defining Characteristics of Highly Effective Leaders

Since the onset of the effective schools movement around 1980, a tremendous amount of research has been accumulated on the actions of effective school leaders. Almost all of this knowledge centers on the functions or tasks with which leaders should be engaged. For example, it is well documented that leaders in productive schools and districts promote and shepherd a vision of education that privileges the success of every child. We also know that these leaders demonstrate the ability to align and integrate the many diverse components of a school or district, especially people, programs, and financial resources.

Over this thirty-five-year time frame, however, little attention has been devoted to uncovering the dynamic characteristics of effective school leaders. The information that we do have is often deeply embedded in the descriptions of leader behaviors. There are reasons for this, of course. One is that behaviors of school leaders historically played second fiddle to leader traits. It is quite appropriate then that actions and tasks now are on center stage. Another is that characteristics have come under heavy attack for being too intangible, too "fluffy," too unteachable, and nonscientific (i.e., not subject to empirical testing).

Work on leadership for school improvement over the last three decades leads me to a different position, however. There is no argument that a tenacious focus on leadership behaviors around the functions of school improvement (e.g., nurturing the development of organizational learning) is essential. I find, however, that there is considerable cost in ignoring or demeaning the characteristics of effective school leaders, ones that have considerable influence in the narrative of school improvement. I discuss four of the most essential of these characteristics in this chapter: passion, persistence, optimism, and authenticity. Collectively, they reflect an essential truth of education: schooling is a human enterprise.

Passion

Deeply engrained in the studies and stories of productive leaders is an often unlabeled theme—one I call passion. Effective school leaders are passionate about the institutions they shepherd. They are passionate about the work they do. And, perhaps most critically, they are passionate about the well being and success of the young people in their care and the teachers who promote that success. Passion plays out differently, of course, with different leaders. But it is never absent in good schools that remain effective year after year. It sounds corny, of course, which I believe helps explain the absence of study on the matter, but passionate leaders see themselves as engaged in something larger and more meaningful than a job or even a profession. Passionate leaders are almost always less ego-centered than their peers. Their dedication and commitment push open opportunities that are often unseen in other schools.

Persistence

This leads naturally to the second characteristic of highly productive school leaders, one again that becomes visible only as we peer behind the front stage of school improvement. Specifically, effective leaders are ferociously persistent in the pursuit of what needs to be done for their schools and districts. It is easy to say that failure is not an option. It is much more difficult to push and pull and carry a school to success. And when we look deeply into the chronicle of school improvement, we see that much of the success we find can be traced back to the commitment to succeed. All of us in the leadership business start out toward the goal of success. However, when we arrive at what seem to be insurmountable barriers, most of us do the natural thing: we turn back or we set up camp where we are. Effective leaders confront these same barriers. However, they do not accept them as inevitable blockages. They are tenacious in helping others find ways to climb over, tunnel under, or carve through barriers.

Optimism

Persistence carries us to the third characteristic of especially effective leaders. These women and men are unrelentingly optimistic. Many of our schools and districts work under a veil of gloom, an inevitable sense that things will not work. The bad things that often befall students become givens, not challenges to be engaged. Schooling becomes a tough slog with little sense of hope. Possibilities seem foreign and unachievable. Damages inflicted on children from the larger world seem impervious to healing efforts. For too many children and their families, success seems a remote possibility at best. However, enmeshed in the mosaic of effective schools and their leaders is a pattern of optimism that becomes visible when we refocus our lenses. When we do so, we see that effective leaders are defined not only by their knowledge and skills with improvement functions (e.g., aligning the curriculum) but also by a powerful sense of optimism. Leaders are diligent in dispelling forces and actions that demean hope. Concomitantly, they are proactive in infusing systems, structures, policies, procedures, and actions that create a culture of possibilities for students and their teachers. They operate from frames of assets, not deficits. These leaders help create schools that our senses tell us are different from the average school. Optimism breeds hope. Hope breeds efficacy. And from all this, schools become places veiled not in gloom but rather the joy of community, engaged work, and accomplishment.

what are the assets?

Authenticity

Entwined in all the evidence of effective leadership is the understanding of principals and superintendents as authentic persons. My finding is not that average leaders are inauthentic, but rather that authenticity as I define it is not a central dynamic in their leadership. Again, when we thoughtfully peer behind the screen of effective leadership behaviors (e.g., using data to inform decision making), we see women and men who are seen by those around them as authentic, caring individuals. They are cloaked in the garb of genuineness. They honor the values that undergird the school and the ethical principles of professionals. Their colleagues and the students view them as trustworthy. They infuse respect into the school as they carry on with their responsibilities. They are people who others tell us can be counted upon to do what they say, what is needed, and what is best for members of the school community.

We close where we began. My purpose here is not to suggest that leadership actions around the instructional program and school culture are less critical today than yesterday. All great schools and effective leaders are marked by strong leadership in these two essential pillars of schools. Rather, my aim is to present the argument based on considerable evidence that when we look deeply into these schools, other elements of effective leadership become distinctly visible. These are the more deeply threaded elements of leadership for school improvement. There are additional constructs that could be highlighted, of course. However, my work leads me to conclude that ideas we examine in this chapter are critical. I refer to them as the four characteristics of effective school leaders: passion, persistence, optimism, and authenticity. I find that they are explanatory in nature. That is, they have a good deal to say about whether leaders can improve schools.

Chapter 5

The 5E Model of School Leadership

For most of the twentieth century, we tended to think about school leadership in certain well-defined ways. We highlighted roles of leaders (e.g., the assistant principal for student services, the associate superintendent for business). We featured academic and student-based domains of responsibility (e.g., department chair, mathematics; assistant superintendent for special education). We also defined leadership in terms of functions (personnel, guidance). And across all of these categories, the spotlight was directed to the tasks of administration (e.g., supervising teachers, communicating with parents). Over the last few decades, as our knowledge of leadership in general and our understanding of school administration in particular have deepened, we have learned that it is more helpful to scaffold school administration on broader crosscutting conceptions of leadership. Here we find that while tasks, roles, responsibilities, and functions continue to help us paint the landscape of school leadership, they become secondary to broad orientations or perspectives that significantly reset the work of the women and men in various school administration positions. In this recast understanding of leadership for the twenty-first century, it makes more sense to talk about empowerment-oriented leadership than it does to talk about school community relations. In a similar vein, it makes more sense to concentrate on learning-focused leadership than it does to talk about supervising and evaluating teachers. Equally important, we find that these core broad orientations or perspectives wrap around, stretch across, or define all administrative positions.

Over the past twenty-five years, my colleagues and I have worked to forge a framework that features these broad, more fundamental, and more essential orientations. Sometimes they can be seen in the background of discussions on leadership for tomorrow's schools. And across this time, colleagues from all domains of the school administration family have turned their lenses on one or more of these orientations. At the same time, comprehensive foundational views of school leadership that provide alternative ways of thinking about who we are and the work we undertake remain rare in our profession. My goal here is to provide some purchase on the transition by sketching out one foundational view of school leadership, what I refer to as the 5E model of school leadership. At the heart of the model are five orientations that define work across tasks, functions, roles, and so forth, orientations that have the potential to give meaning to and bring coherence to the complex and multi-faceted nature of school administration. The model, I believe, helps recenter the work of those who lead our schools.

Figure 5.1   The 5E Model of Leadership

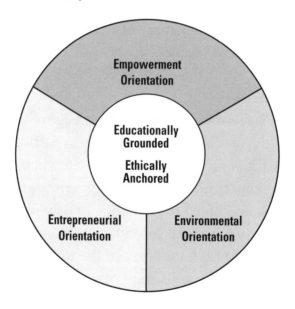

Educational Leadership

As you can see in Figure 5.1, the model defines leadership in terms of five core orientations, perspectives that an abundance of recent evidence helps us understand are at the center of effective management and high-performing organizations. At the heart of the framework are two key pillars that provide the central support structure of school leadership in a post-industrial world and, in the process, give meaning to the other three orientations.

To switch metaphors, the 5E model tells us that school leaders need glasses with orientations (not tasks) and that the lenses in these spectacles should direct attention to the educational and moral aspects of schooling. Using the educational lens, the model tells us that the ground for administration must be learning, teaching, and school improvement (i.e., education)— not organization, politics, administration, or governance. These latter issues are important, often critically so, but only in the service of strengthening the educational program at the school or district, not as center-stage players in the educational drama. The framework tells us that a key to great leadership is the ability to throw the educational spotlight on the hundreds and hundreds of decisions that school leaders make every day—that is, not to allow decisions to be consummated primarily on organizational, financial, and political grounds.

Ethical Leadership

The center of the model also shows us that effective leadership grows from the seedbed of ethics, the ethics of care and justice in particular. While the demands for scientifically based evidence are important, school leaders, the model tells us, must also build their leadership on a robust platform of values. While there is, to be sure, some scientific information about programs that might provide an advantage to children from poor communities, there is no science that tells leaders that enhanced student performance should be pursued by reaching out to the underserved. We have had scientific evidence for decades about how to close achievement gaps and hold students from low-income families in school. The problem was less a lack of evidence than it was a lack of willingness to challenge the moral bankruptcy of organizational routines (e.g., the ways students were grouped for instruction, the guidance that low-income families received, the methods used to assign teachers to students, and so forth). Thus, the model tells us that one lens of leaders' spectacles must direct attention to the moral implications of the routine decisions, practices, behaviors, structures, and policies that engage school leaders—regardless of their roles, tasks, or areas of responsibility.

Empowering Leadership

The other three Es in the model also help to reforge the meaning of school leadership. Schools in the United States were built up from raw material provided by organizational and institutional conceptions of schooling. The school administration literature from throughout the twentieth century is replete with discussions of hierarchical and bureaucratic pillars of management (e.g., authority, control, impersonality, division of labor, and so forth). Contrary to what is increasingly portrayed, hierarchy and bureaucracy are not a priori evil twins. In many fundamental ways, they provide the structure and glue to hold schools and school systems together. The problem emerges when they occupy center stage rather than a supporting role. The 5E model helps us see that these basics of schooling must be yoked to larger purposes and goals, that we can no longer allow them to distort education for youngsters and communities of students and adults. It tells us that a primary focus on hierarchy and administrative control will fail schools much more frequently than it helps. It tells us that leadership, whether by an assistant principal or director of assessment, is about empowering others—providing direction, building capacity, removing barriers, and so forth—to carry the school to more productive places.

Entrepreneurial Leadership

The fourth E in the model informs us that effective school leadership must maintain an entrepreneurial orientation, if not by predilection then by stint of serious training. We know that the entire foundation of schooling in the United States is being reshaped using forms that privilege markets and clients, ideas that were largely conspicuous by their absence even twenty years ago. The public monopoly with its domination by the providers of education services has given way and is continuing to be replaced by systems that honor customers and clients, as well as professional expertise and government control. As we continue building with these forms, it is imperative, the model asserts, that administrators learn and practice the art of entrepreneurship—risk taking, innovativeness, and proactiveness, elements that have rarely defined a field dominated by concern for roles, responsibilities, and tasks.

Environmental Leadership

Finally, the 5E model tells us that school leadership needs to be rooted as much in understanding the environment as the internal operations of schools. While always somewhat "open" to the larger environment, the current era of accountability, marketization, and community has made an orientation of environmental sensitivity increasingly more critical. And, I argue, this orientation is more important than many of the ways of thinking about leadership that dominated the practice and academic domains of school administration for most of the twentieth century.

In closing, we end where we started. Leaders today, regardless of role or function or task, need broader and more powerful ways to think about who they are and what they do. Older ways of conceptualizing leadership and describing their efforts will not disappear. But, I believe, they must come to occupy less of the stage in the school leadership play. More important, they will continue to be of use when they are informed by more powerful leadership orientations. One such set of orientations can be found in the 5E model of leadership.

Part 2

Focusing the Lens on School Improvement

Getting to Know

dance and music
logic and numbers
stories, tales, parables, and metaphors
imagination, feelings, and intuition
belief and hope
caring and touch

Chapter 6

Beyond the Factors:
The Threads of School Improvement

School improvement is primarily about the "stuff" that needs to be addressed. Over the years, the "goods" have been called correlates, factors, elements, ingredients, and so on. At the same time, school improvement is about conditions and supports that both link elements and provide some of the fuel for them to work well, conditions that lurk in the background of the school improvement narrative. In this chapter, because leadership for school improvement requires a clear understanding of and ability to work with what I call the threads of change, I pull these conditions and supports from the background and put them on center stage. I start with some guidelines about the road to school improvement and move on to analyses of three supporting concepts: collective, multifaceted work; context; and coherence. It is important to begin with an acknowledgment that there is considerable overlap among these supports and conditions.

Major figures in the study of organizational change and school improvement have described the school improvement pathway as uneven and full of unexpected twists and turns. Scholars in these domains portray change as evolutionary as well as planful. The voyage is marked by starts, retreats, and starts again.

In particular, analysts have discovered that school improvement work, especially in schools with large numbers of students at risk, is often characterized by increased tensions, the unsettling of comfortable routines, cultural resistance, new enactments of micropolitical behavior, and the surfacing of concerns. Thus, they document that change is often accompanied by an implementation dip. Things are likely to trend downward, both in human terms, such as confidence and morale, and performance, before they turn upward.

Relatedly, we learn that success is fragile. Victory is hardly inevitable and once garnered requires some vigilance to maintain. Turnover of personnel is often accompanied by regression. Energy naturally leaks out of the system, and the loss is often unnoticed or, if detected, not replenished. The environments in which schools find themselves are always evolving, pushing one reform forward only to be replaced by another a short time later. Mandates proliferate, overload sets in, fragmentation increases, meaning dissipates, and people withdraw to the safety of the past and the comforts of old routines. Change becomes a ritual that washes over the school. Sustainability is undermined.

Collective, Multifaceted Work

One of the most important understandings that has emerged from the broad field of school improvement, especially improvement for students placed at risk, is that troubles and problems are traceable to the broader society in which schools are nested. Therefore, school improvement efforts must extend beyond the school. This means collective work. To start, it means a larger role for nonschool agencies in reshaping the political, economic, social, and cultural forces that disadvantage many children. Second, it suggests that schools and other institutions and systems of support need to work in tandem. None alone are likely to be successful, especially when improvement means turning around troubled situations. Third, it necessitates greater efforts on the part of schools to extend their work beyond the traditional boundaries of schooling, to take ownership for a wider array of services.

We have also learned over the years that there is no single factor, element, or component that will lead to dramatic school improvement. What is required is a collective attack. A productive school improvement design would be comprehensive, providing a combination of elements. It would provide significant initiatives on a number of fronts (i.e., be multilayered and multitiered). As I discuss in detail in the following paragraphs, the design would be interconnected, aligned, integrated, and coordinated. It would attend to both the short and long term. It would offer redundancy.

The chronicle on multistrand school improvement work contains a number of key subthemes. We know, for example, that there are some components that are necessary not because they push the needle forward but because their absence can derail the rest of the bundle of work. A safe and orderly learning environment falls into this category.

We also know that weaknesses in any of the key pieces of the overall design make improvement problematic; each element needs to reach at least the moderate level of effectiveness. Additionally, there is some evidence of a multiplier effect in play. "A" may be weak by itself, as might "B." Together, however, they might produce a moderate to strong effect. It is a combination of small effects working together that make a difference.

Studies of school improvement with nearly every group of students at risk inform us that the more disadvantaged the population the more effort is needed to reach and the more constant that work must be. For example, while middle-class school communities benefit from school improvement ingredients measuring at mid-level strengths, only high strength leads to improvement in at-risk communities.

Researchers have also uncovered another dimension of the multiple factor law. As I underscore throughout the book, for students placed at risk both academic and cultural levers need to be engaged.

There is emerging evidence that the multifactor package of school improvement components for children placed at risk must avoid pivoting heavily on remediation. Successful work requires simultaneous movement on both helping youngsters catch up and keeping them in sync with their classmates. An effective design needs to include both remediation and acceleration. The corollaries are that (1) early intervention efforts almost always trump later work and (2) prevention of problems trumps remediation of problems.

Some of the most important sublessons threaded into the role of collectivism in school improvement research address issues of time. We learn, for example, that sufficient time to get reforms germinated is quite important. We also learn from studies and integrative reviews that it takes considerable time for improvement initiatives to flower. An analog in this story is that, in general, improvement is developmental: it appears gradually and incrementally.

Success is by no means assured in the school improvement game, especially when situations and environments are turbulent and when schools are in troubled condition. Because of this, and for substantive and symbolic reasons, small wins over time are heralded in the school improvement literature, especially for schools that underserved youth attend. These small impacts are often quite meaningful.

An important but less developed time theme is that some interventions play out differently across the careers of students. For example, teacher expectations carry more weight with younger students. Other time themes were noted previously: early is better than later and prevention trumps remediation.

Culture and Seedbeds

Perhaps the most essential threaded law that leaders and policy makers need to burn into their minds is that structural changes do not predict organizational outcomes. Numerous studies and reviews have affirmed this fact over the last quarter century in nearly every domain of schooling, and nearly every researcher, developer, and school leader has been frustrated by this truth. Additionally, what holds for structures holds for resources and policies as well. This is particularly unsettling knowledge because leaders have been inculcated to rely on structural change to power reform. Additionally, for reasons that Elmore (1995) explains in his classic essay (i.e., ease of use and high symbolic value), policy makers and other reformers routinely perpetuate the logic and practice of structural change.

Four lines of explanation shed light on the disconnect between structure and school improvement. One focuses on the fact that structures are a long way from outcomes: the path between macro-level reconfigurations and micro-level processes and activities is long, many-jointed, and loosely linked in a number of places. Structures need to produce changes in the conditions of learning if they are to be successful. However, it is a problematic bet that they can do so. For example, moving from a regular schedule to a blocked one does nothing to change the quality of instruction or the robustness of the curriculum in classrooms. Advisory periods are as likely to be sterile as they are to foster personalization.

A second line of analysis concludes that schools are characterized by deep patterns of who they are and how they do the business of education.

Structural patterns that are inconsistent with the existing grammar of schooling routinely fail to produce desired change. The existing conditions, if you will, almost always cause new ideas to conform to the prevailing ideology rather than shape it. As Fullan has reminded us for the last thirty years, culture needs to change to make structures viable.

Third, there is considerable evidence that structural changes are often introduced with little sensitivity to the local context or situation in the school, regardless of whether there is congruence with the prevailing culture. We examine this essential supporting condition in the following paragraphs.

Finally, schools are generally subject to the mistaken belief that the "goods" they want to import are an integral part of the structure they are inviting in (e.g., "community" always accompanies structural changes in the size of a school). The problem is that the assumption is false. The result is that the structure is imported but the DNA that made it work elsewhere is not. Schools end up with structural shells—empty forms—that do not power school improvement.

The great paradox here is that while reworking the culture, or the seed-bed, of the school is the main work, structural changes are required to hold new cultural patterns and understandings in place. That is, while structures have only limited influence on culture and conditions that enhance learning, without them new cultural perspectives will dissipate.

Context

School improvement sleuths examining every aspect of change arrive at the conclusion that, regardless of the "reform agenda," context is a cardinal, but not determinate, variable in the change growth process. Context helps set the rules and norms as well as the constraints that shape improvement work. Because situations are idiosyncratic, reforms must be molded to fit the context at hand.

To begin with, it is important to remember that government context can heavily influence school-based improvement work—for better or worse. Relatedly, a massive amount of evidence has accumulated that community contexts create powerful forces that can bolster or hinder improvement initiatives. SES, ethnicity, language, housing conditions, urbanicity, history, and so forth all matter.

Classroom contexts exert considerable pull over improvement efforts as well. Teachers bring their own cultural understandings, skills, and backgrounds to the job. Each develops a grammar of instruction that has an impact on how each teacher views and engages with change. The importance of teacher as person-in-situation is an important theme that is often overlooked in bringing school improvement correlates to life. For example, investigators often report that younger teachers with fewer years of experience are more apt to actively engage in reform efforts. Subject matter taught and department affiliation also have a role in this chronicle.

School context also influences the viability and meaningfulness of improvement efforts, both directly and through the way it shapes activities in classrooms and the sensemaking of individuals. We know, for example, that "level" often produces different interpretations of change efforts. Geographical location has been found to be influential. So too has the health of a school and the extent of the challenges it confronts—that is, where it falls on the continuum from troubled to highly effective. The high student mobility that characterizes schools with a preponderance of students placed at risk also shapes school improvement efforts. Because youngsters from different environments view education and schooling in different ways, the demographics of the student body are regularly uncovered as school-level contextual variables that influence school improvement work. The nature of the community of adults in the schools is also consequential, especially the nature of relationships in place.

The fact that context matters, and that it matters a good deal, has implications for policy makers, researchers, developers, and practitioners. However, an important caveat needs to surface. To maintain, as we do throughout this book, that context is important is not the same thing as arguing that it is determinate, and understanding does not require educators to be held hostage to context. Also, to underscore the importance of the situation does not mean that generalized reform ideas are dead on arrival. The notion that all school reforms need to be completely homegrown is scientifically unjustified. The objective is flexibility to meet or adapt to local conditions.

At the same time, members of the educational family need to acknowledge the place of situation when working with the correlates of school improvement and understand that reform does not occur in a vacuum. They need to learn that context is not simply a box for reform but an essential aspect of the work itself. Included here is the understanding that what works easily or smoothly in one school may require the investment of considerable capital and energy in another school. It also means acting in ways that honor the limitations of telling and mandating as engines of school improvement. Improvements have to play out at the street level. While the prize is never abandoned, localization and customization are needed (and appropriate) to gain it. Strategies and correlates must be formed to fit the situation while working simultaneously to influence context in directions that support improvement. Adaptation will be the norm. Policy makers, researchers, developers, and practitioners also need to be cognizant of the fact that this adaptive school improvement work is likely to produce unintended consequences.

Coherence

Building on the findings from the pioneers in the effective schools movement, we distilled consistency, coordination, integration, and alignment (i.e., coherence) as one of the essential beams supporting the correlates of highly productive schools. More important, analysts peering in on successful practice have unearthed the dimensions or essential aspects of coherence:

- integrating within each component of school improvement work
- aligning across subject areas (e.g., a single point of view about writing across all academic domains)
- integrating between and among components of the work (e.g., between mission/goals and professional development)
- coordinating the four pieces of the instructional program—standards, instruction, curriculum, and assessment
- working as a collective rather than discrete set of individual actors
- abandoning practices and policies that get in the way of improvement, that foster fragmentation and overload
- keeping the core issues at the center, maintaining a ferocious focus on what counts
- shaping influences from beyond the organization (e.g., the state, the community) to fit the school context and goals

- cascading improvement efforts and values across organizational levels (e.g., district-school-classroom), not isolating them to a single area

- employing resources in an integrated manner, especially personnel

- getting organizational policies, structures, and operating systems to operate in tandem and in mutually reinforcing ways (e.g., around time usage)

- building redundancy into improvement work

- aligning the formal and informal aspects of the organization

- filtering discordant messages and demands

- shaping the sensemaking frames that hold the high ground in the school

- linking short- and long-term perspectives

- thoroughly compressing variability in the academic program and the school culture

- creating integration between school and work

We close our discussion of alignment and coordination with an important reminder. At the school level, it is the principal who is the prime actor in the coherence narrative, the one who wields the tools to forge integration. For a variety of reasons, coherence is not a natural state in schools. Things are more likely to pull apart than cohere. Alignment, integration, and cohesion require a strong hand.

Most of the work in the area of school improvement by policy makers, researchers, developers, and practitioners focuses on the content of good schools. This is quite natural and has produced robust sets of elements or ingredients for schools where all students reach ambitious targets of performance. At the same time, research over the last thirty years leads me to conclude that there are powerful conditions and supports that are essential to make the factors function well. These conditions are often found deeply embedded in studies of school improvement and are ribboned across the stories. In this chapter, we pulled these threads onto center stage, highlighting three of the most critical chains across the correlates: collective, multifaceted work; context; and coherence.

Chapter 7

Understanding School Improvement

In this chapter, I would like us to explore what we mean when we talk about school improvement, exposing the central reality that school improvement needs to be understood in terms of the larger political, social, and economic forces in play at any given time. I also suggest that our understanding of school improvement is defined by changes in the center of gravity within the education industry itself. That is, it is only by discerning major changes in what counts as schooling, changes influenced by larger economic, political, and social forces, that we know what school improvement means. In short, the construct of school improvement has varied over time. At the end of this chapter, the reader should have a good understanding of the seedbed from which current efforts at school improvement grow—and why those efforts look the way they do.

In this chapter, I also review what scholars have uncovered about how to build productive schools in a post-industrial world. I present this as a framework for school improvement work. I begin with the basic equation of school improvement, and then deepen the narrative around that essential algorithm. I accomplish this by exposing and populating the key dimensions of the school improvement framework: the building material, construction principles, supporting frames, and integrative dynamic.

The General Orientation

Over the last few decades, I have combined two frames to hammer out a way to think broadly about the evolution and growth of school improvement. One frame is historical analysis, studying school improvement over long stretches of time. The other frame is Tushman and Romanelli's (1985) seminal theory of organizational evolution, the punctuated equilibrium model of organizational change. The historical analysis provides the content of the narrative; the punctuated equilibrium model provides the frames to make sense of that content.

At the heart of their model, Tushman and Romanelli hypothesize that "organizations progress through *convergent* periods punctuated by *reorientations* which demark and set the bearings for the next convergent period" (p. 173). According to the theory, convergent periods cover long time spans during which incremental and marginal shifts that refine and elaborate organizational elements toward increased alignment dominate. Reorientations, on the other hand, encompass "periods of discontinuous change where strategies, power, structure, and systems are fundamentally transformed toward a new basis of alignment" (p. 173). According to the model, the critical driver of fundamental change is upheaval in the environment of the institution. In particular, the punctuated equilibrium theory of organizational evolution posits that two forces provide the impetus for change in institutions—that is, for punctuating a reorientation that disrupts a period of convergence: (1) a track record of low performance and (2) fundamental shifts in the environment surrounding an institution that make existing arrangements increasingly ineffective. Tushman and Romanelli maintain that shock from the environment can be addressed either through anticipatory actions or skilled work after impact, and that the internal dimensions of the organization can be brought into congruence with external forces. They maintain that effective or improving organizations are those that create this alignment. They and other scholars also routinely find that leadership mediates, effectively or ineffectively, between internal forces promoting inertia and the demands for fundamental change that emanate from the environment.

When we bring our two frames together in education, we learn that our industry has indeed experienced long eras of convergence followed by much shorter periods of reorientation. We have been pushed out of convergence (or into reorientation) by external changes in the environment (i.e., by economic, political, and social forces). We also see that "what counts" for school improvement changes during these periods of transition and solidifies as new eras of convergence firm up.

Peering a bit more deeply, we learn that we are in a period of reorientation at the current time (1990→), being pushed from a long era of convergence (1920–1990). We see also that consistent with the punctuated equilibrium model forces external to education are powering much of the unsettling of the status quo.

To begin with, it is almost a fundamental law that the economy is undergoing a significant metamorphosis. There is widespread agreement that we have been and continue to be moving from an industrial to a post-industrial or information economy. Key aspects of the new economy include the globalization of economic activity, the demise of the mass-production economy, a privileging of information technology, an increase in the skills required to be successful, and an emphasis on the service dimensions of the marketplace. It is also becoming clear to many analysts that with the arrival of the post-industrial society, we are experiencing a breakdown of the social structure associated with industrialism. The ascent of the global economy has brought an emphasis on new markets. Supported by market theory and theories of the firm and by the public choice literature, there is a renewed interest in private market.

The political and social environments also appear to be undergoing important changes. There has been a loosening of bonds of democracy. The infrastructure of civil society also has been impaired. Analysts discern fairly significant tears in the fabric known as modern civil society. As a consequence of these basic shifts—the weakening of democracy and the deterioration of civil society, especially in conjunction with the ideological space they share with economic fundamentalism—important sociopolitical trends have begun to emerge: (1) an increasing sense of personal insecurity and unease in the population at large; (2) the deterioration of essential features of community life; (3) shifts in the boundaries—both real and symbolic—between the state and alternative sociopolitical structures; and (4) an expanding belief that the enhancement of social justice through collective action, especially public action, is unlikely.

One strand of this evolving sociopolitical mosaic is plummeting public support for government. Citizens are becoming disconnected from and frustrated with government and politics. They lack faith in public officials, and they are skeptical of the bureaucratic quagmire of professional control that defined education for almost all of the twentieth century.

The ideological footings of the emerging sociopolitical infrastructure are also becoming increasingly visible. The one piece of the foundation that shines most brightly is a high regard for individualism and liberty, both of which honor the individual and discredit collective action. It includes the privileging of private over public delivery and a diminution in the power of government agents and professional experts.

The Shifting Dynamics of Education

As I have documented over the last quarter century, school improvement in a post-industrial educational world looks differently than it did during the long era of convergence between 1920 and 1990. I see the reforged concept in each of the three critical domains of schools: goals and the core technology, management and organization, and linkages to external constituents (the institutional level).

There is some evidence that a more robust understanding of the education production function is beginning to be translated into new ways of thinking about learning and teaching. Indeed, a century of focus on teaching is giving way to a focus on learning. In addition, the strongest theoretical and disciplinary influence on education—behavioral psychology—is being supplemented by constructivist psychology and newer sociological perspectives on learning—in much the same way that behavioral psychology pushed mind psychology aside in the early 1900s. This shift toward research on cognition and learning offers quite different understandings of school improvement work. Underlying these changes are profoundly different ways of thinking about the educability of children. Those at the forefront of this reorientation away from schools that were historically organized to produce results consistent with the normal curve, to sort youth into the various strata needed to fuel the economy, see education being transformed around a new definition of equal opportunity for learners—equal access to high-status knowledge.

At the organizational level, reorientation has thrown into question the operant organizational and management models and structures of the twentieth century. There is a growing sentiment that the existing administrative structure is failing. It is increasingly being concluded that the existing bureaucratic system of administration is incapable of addressing the needs of a post-industrial education system.

In particular, the institutional and hierarchical system of management has come under sharp criticism from (1) those who argue that schools are so covered with bureaucratic sediment that initiative, creativity, and professional judgment have all been paralyzed and the likely success of reforms has been neutralized; (2) critics who maintain that bureaucratic management practices are interfering with learning; (3) analysts who believe that bureaucracy is counterproductive to the needs and interests of educators within schools; (4) critics who suggest that bureaucratic management is inconsistent with the sacred values of education; (5) scholars who view bureaucracy as a form of operation that inherently forces attention away from the core technology of schooling; (6) reform proponents who hold that the existing organizational structure of schools is neither sufficiently flexible nor sufficiently robust to meet the needs of students in a post-industrial society; and (7) analysts who believe that the rigidities of bureaucracy impede the ability of parents and citizens to govern and reform schooling.

This tremendous attack on the institutional and bureaucratic infrastructure of schools has led to alternative methods of operating that are grounded on new values and principles. Concomitantly, new forms of school organization and management are emerging. The basic organizing and management principles of schooling are giving way to more proactive attempts to lead educational systems. Forms to significantly change the nature of social relationships in schools are emerging. The hierarchical, bureaucratic organizational structures that have defined schools since the onslaught of scientific management in the early 1900s are giving way to more decentralized and more professionally controlled systems that create new designs for school management. In these new post-industrial organizations, there are important shifts in roles, relationships, and responsibilities: traditional patterns of relationships are altered, authority flows are less hierarchical, role definitions are both more general and more flexible, leadership is connected to competence for needed tasks rather than to formal position, and independence and isolation are replaced by cooperative work. Furthermore, the structural orientation implanted during the reign of scientific management is being overshadowed by a focus on the human element. The operant goal is no longer maintenance of the organizational infrastructure but rather the development of human resources. Learning climates and organizational adaptivity are being substituted for the more traditional emphasis on uncovering and applying the one best model of performance.

Most analysts of the institutional level of schooling—the interface of the school with its larger environment—have concluded that the public monopoly approach to education is being recast at the current time (i.e., during the current period of reorientation). They envision the demise of schooling as a sheltered government monopoly heavily controlled by professionals. In its stead, they forecast the emergence of a system of schooling and improvement designs driven by economic and political forces that substantially increase the saliency of the market. Embedded in this conception are a number of interesting dynamics, all of which gain force from a realignment of power and influence between professional educators and consumers. The most important is that the traditional dominant relationship—with professional educators on the playing field and parents on the sidelines acting as cheerleaders, agitators, or, more likely, passive spectators—is replaced by rules that advantage the consumer.

Four elements of this emerging portrait of transformed governance for consumers are most prevalent: choice in selecting a school, voice in school governance, partnership in the education of their children, and enhanced membership in the school community. Central to all four is a blurring of the boundaries between the home and the school, between the school and the community, and between professional staff and lay constituents. Collectively, these components lend support to the grassroots political and competitive economic arguments that support the calls for more locally controlled organizations and to market-anchored conceptions of school improvement.

> In this chapter, I provided a robust treatment of the meaning of school improvement in the post-industrial world of education. I undertook this exploration because it is foundational to school improvement work yet receives only passing notice, at best, in the literature. School improvement, we saw, is not a fixed concept. It takes on different meanings in different times. I argued that current perspectives on school improvement have been heavily shaped by powerful forces external to the business of education as well as an ongoing reorientation of schooling that is pushing the profession off the footings on which it sat for almost all of the twentieth century.

Chapter 8

The Architecture of School Improvement

For more than forty years, beginning with the early teacher effects and school effectiveness studies, academics, practitioners, developers, and policy makers have been struggling with the task of building good schools. During that time, we have passed through different eras of school improvement work, such as effective schools, systemic school improvement, school restructuring, comprehensive school reform, school turnaround, scaling up, and so forth. We have been supplied with an amazing variety of specific interventions designed to assist educators in helping all students achieve ambitious targets of performance. Over that time, I have been engaged in accumulating and making sense of all that work. My colleagues and I have reaffirmed some well-accepted cannons of school improvement and added layers of depth to others. We have also uncovered some new insights about dimensions of school improvement that have been insufficiently investigated. But most important, I believe that we have created a comprehensive and integrated way to think about and then build productive schools—what we call the architecture of school improvement.

A Framework for School Improvement

As noted in the introduction, our assignment in this section, our goal if you will, is to present a way of thinking about school improvement that both honors our re-oriented view of education and grounds its conclusions on the best empirical evidence from the last three decades. I lay out a framework that accomplishes this in five parts: an essential equation, building material, construction principles, enabling supports, and integrative device (see Figure 8.1).

Figure 8.1   The Architecture of School Improvement

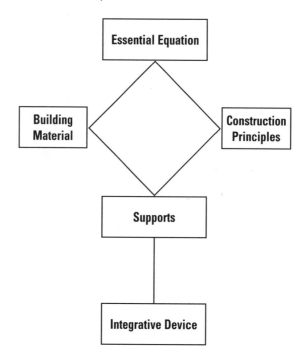

Essential Equation

Collectively, the evidence directs me to the position that there is an essential school improvement algorithm, one that is both simple and elegant:

School Improvement = Academic Press + Supportive Community

The equation represents the core of school improvement work in the modern era. Another parsimonious model for this narrative is the double helix. Both encapsulations inform us that (1) these are the two critical components of school improvement, (2) they are most powerful in tandem, and (3) they work best when they wrap around each other like strands in a rope.

The questions at hand are: How can academic press and supportive culture be created in schools? How can school improvement be realized? My work over the years has convinced me that the answer is contained in the other four pieces of the framework.

Building Material

The first of these pieces, the content, involves identifying and bringing the right materials to the school improvement building site. This is the

Go to **www.learningsciences.com/bookresources** to download figures and tables.

aspect of the framework that has been most deeply explored over the last three decades. During that time, researchers were quite active in mining for the raw materials of school improvement. In addition, using these materials, numerous content-based taxonomies have been forged, beginning around 1980 with the correlates of effective schools and carrying through to today as seen in the recent comprehensive review of meta-analyses by Hattie (2009) and the hallmark study by Bryk and colleagues (2010) on the essential elements of school improvement (see Table 8.1).

Table 8.1   The Building Material of School Improvement

Quality Instruction
- Effective teachers
- Quality pedagogy

Curriculum
- Content coverage
- Time
- Rigor
- Relevance

Personalized Learning Environment for Students
- Safe and orderly climate
- Meaningful connections
- Opportunities to participate

Professional Learning Environment for Educators
- Collaborative culture of work
- Participation and ownership
- Shared leadership

Learning-Centered Leadership
- Forging academic press
- Developing supportive culture

Learning-Centered Linkages to the School Community
- Connections to parents
- Linkages to community agencies and organizations

Monitoring of Progress and Performance Accountability
- Performance-based goals
- Systematic used of data
- Shared accountability

The good news here is that while lists and taxonomies often feature different terms and place ideas in different categories, there is an astonishing amount of agreement on the material contained in these categorizations, on the ingredients of school improvement, that is. It is beyond the scope of this chapter to provide a comprehensive and integrative analysis of thirty years of scholarship. Rather, based on that work, I simply offer a taxonomy constructed from those studies, one that captures the "right stuff" of school improvement—the content with the potential to create academic press and supportive culture. This particular taxonomy is a refinement of my efforts in this area beginning in the 1980s and carrying through 2013.

Construction Principles

While attention has been lavished on uncovering the best materials (content) to use to forge school improvement initiatives—that is, to help create schools defined by academic press and supportive culture—our understanding of the rules that need to be followed in putting the content pieces together is much less well developed. What we do know is often embedded in or threaded across the content narrative. Principles rarely have a starring role in the school improvement play. One often has to read between the lines to discover these ideas. The art of "seeing the missing" is also essential in developing an understanding of these guiding principles. Forensic school improvement work is generally a good method of identifying the pieces of this critical component of the school improvement framework.

Based on a close reading of school improvement research over a long period of time, my assessment mirrors that of Michael Fullan (1982, 2002)—that is, the construction principles are as important as the content elements in school improvement work. Working on the latter without attending to the former is a recipe for failure, akin to building beautiful rooms on the third floor of a house without load-bearing walls. While it is beyond the scope of this chapter to compile and describe the universe of these principles, given the impoverished state of knowledge in this area of the framework, simply providing a taxonomy is insufficient. Instead, I illustrate the idea of "construction principles" with three examples.

Structure Does Not Predict Performance. Almost all school improvement work involves structural changes. This is appropriate, for as Kirst and Meister (1985) documented in their cardinal analysis, structural changes are needed to capture and hold reform initiatives. However, the prevalent assumption that structure (e.g., block scheduling) will provide desired results (e.g., better instruction, more student engagement) is without foundation. We see the essential paradox of school improvement construction work: structural changes almost never predict outcomes, but they are essential for initiatives to take root and develop.

Here is the essence of the problem. Educators, in their attempts to improve their schools, identify activities that worked elsewhere and then bring them home. These are almost universally structural transfers (e.g., academies, looping, charter schools, ungraded classrooms, detracking, and so forth). School leaders are often masters at brokering such transfers. Policy at all levels bolsters this approach to school improvement as well. The disheartening reality is that the DNA of these interventions (i.e., what made them work elsewhere) rarely makes the voyage as the structures are transferred. What schools end up with are empty shells of change, structures without the fuel to power improvement.

Another encapsulation of the structural principle is that form follows function. Or alternatively, school improvement work is first and foremost about identifying the DNA of improvement, then building out structures to contain that material. Violation of this construction principle is the norm in schools. It dooms a good deal of all improvement work, much more so than the selection of the wrong building materials.

Context Always Matters. Research from every sector of the school reform landscape confirms that context is critical. History and experience, type of school, nature of the community and the district, level of schooling, and an assortment of other contextual factors are important in the development of academic press and supportive culture. For example, creating personalized learning environments is somewhat different work in high schools than in elementary schools. Interventions, built or imported (even when they carry the right DNA), need to be shaped and contoured to fit the school context. When they are not, they tend not to fit. And when improvement efforts do not fit at the school, they rarely flourish.

Cohesion and Alignment Are Essential. Two decades ago, Richard Elmore (1995) first helped me understand the meaning of cohesion in school improvement work when he noted that pretty much anything (from the right content categories) done well will work. Since that time, other scholars have added some nuances to this important lesson and helped form it into an essential school improvement construction principle. Creating separate galaxies for content elements and their related anchor programs is a poor way to pursue school improvement. The better approach, and the only one with real hope of promoting successful change, is to bring whatever content is engaged into one galaxy with a common center of gravity. Employing building materials that are of medium quality (i.e., has only medium effect sizes) but that are universally supported and richly linked to other elements in the school will ensure greater improvement than using high-quality content elements that are poorly connected.

We close this section by returning to the core message: construction principles are an essential component of the school improvement framework. Yet they receive only limited attention in scholarly analysis and are often conspicuous by their absence from school improvement work. This fact explains the failure of school improvement efforts to a much greater extent than do poor choices in selecting building materials.

Supports

We have also learned, again from examining embedded patterns in the school improvement mosaic, that organizational tools need to be thoughtfully used if school improvement efforts are to bear fruit. They are the fourth component of the framework.

All of the building materials and guiding principles by definition carry a positive charge. Each is a hero or heroine in the school improvement narrative—although, as noted previously, with limited powers when working alone. Organizational supports, on the other hand, are neutral. They can carry either a positive or a negative charge; that is, they can be employed to help or hinder school improvement work.

There are a variety of ways to think about these supports or tools. For example, there is the well-established framework of "capital": human capital, financial capital, social capital, and so forth, with each form of capital comprised of numerous subdimensions (e.g., leadership capital in the human capital area). However, in employing the idea of neutral charge, we underscore a design that is more compact and considerably less likely to bleed into "material" and "principles" than other support taxonomies. Here we include organizational structures (e.g., grade-level academies, K–2 schools), operating systems (e.g., procedures for assigning children to teachers and classes), policies (e.g., assigning struggling students to mandatory after-school tutoring), and practices (e.g., the way the principal interacts with children in the school hallways). We find considerable evidence in the school improvement research that the tools to mix quality material and construction principles in a productive fashion are found in these categories.

The Integrative Dynamic

Since the first studies of effective schools and districts and investigations of successful change, leadership has enjoyed a central role in the school improvement narrative. It is prominently displayed in Table 8.1, mentioned previously. My work with my colleague, Philip Hallinger, over the last thirty years has taken me beyond that conclusion, however. I see a deeper pattern of leadership in the school improvement tapestry, and a more central location for that pattern. The storyline is one in which school leaders provide the dynamism to make all the components of the framework function. The recent cardinal volume by Bryk and colleagues (2010) affirms leadership as the integrative dynamic. More specifically, they conclude that leadership is the essential enabling element of school improvement work.

We then exposed the architecture that captures the universe of school improvement, or alternatively, the scaffolding that undergirds all effective improvement efforts. At the heart of that framework is the essential school improvement equation, one that defines school improvement as academic press and supportive culture. We saw that concepts and materials from the other components of the framework come together to energize the essential equation. We discussed the component that is best understood, the content of school improvement or the right building material. Here I argued that a near myopic focus on content has limited our ability to secure the end goal of improvement. I then introduced the third component of the framework, school improvement construction principles. I reported that the inability to understand and operationalize these principles has been largely responsible for the frustration and ineffectiveness of much school improvement work. A parsimonious and neutrally charged set of the tools that need to be used in school improvement work was then layered into the framework. We closed with the empirically anchored conclusion that leadership is the integrative dynamic in fostering school improvement.

Part 3

Focusing the Lens on Leadership for School Improvement

A Good School

A wagon team of adventure
each cart freighted with the mundane made magical
each driven by an expectant guide
each trailer brandishing a certificate of membership

The caravan traveling toward distant portals of possibility,
defenders of care on every horizon, guarding each passageway
wagons awash in the glow of hope

Uncharted landscape collectively explored
navigational challenges falling to communal labors

Distinctive tags of friendship decorating each backpack
badges of accomplishments proudly displayed, joyfully celebrated

Chapter 9

Leadership for Learning

(with Mark Smylie and Karen Seashore Louis)

Over the last half century, a great deal has been written about the importance of leadership, in general and in relation to organizational performance in particular. Academics, practitioners, and reviewers from every field of study have concluded that leadership is a central variable in the equation that defines organizational success. Looking specifically at education, we have parallel evidence that leadership is a central ingredient—and often the keystone element—in school and district success as defined in terms of student achievement.

An assortment of researchers over the last three decades has helped us see that not all leadership is equal, that a particular type of leadership is especially visible in high-performing schools and school districts. This type of leadership can best be labeled "leadership for learning," "instructionally focused leadership," or "leadership for school improvement." The touchstones for this type of leadership include the ability of leaders to (1) stay consistently focused on the right stuff—learning, teaching, curriculum and assessment, and the school culture—and (2) make all the other dimensions of schooling (e.g., administration, organization, finance) work in the service of learning.

Our model of leading the instructional program is presented in Figure 9.1. We begin at the left-hand side of the model, where we observe that the leadership behaviors are heavily shaped by four major conditions: (1) the previous experiences of a leader (e.g., experience as a curriculum coordinator in a district office will probably lead to the use of behaviors different from those featured by a leader who has had considerable experience as an assistant principal for discipline); (2) the knowledge base the leader amasses over time; (3) the types of personal characteristics a leader brings to the job (e.g., achievement need, energy level); and (4) the set of values and beliefs that help define a leader (e.g., beliefs regarding the appropriate role for subordinates in decision processes). Consistent with the best literature in this area, we see that the impact of leadership behaviors in terms of valued outcomes is indirect. That is, it is mediated by school operations and classroom activities. Or, more to the point, leaders influence the factors that, in turn, influence the outcomes (e.g., student graduation).

Figure 9.1   Learning-Centered Leadership Framework

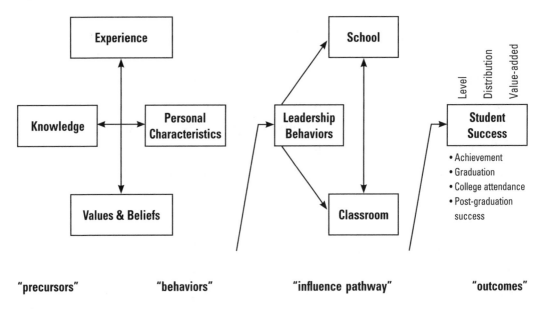

There are four major dimensions of behavior that characterize leadership of the instructional program. Each of these dimensions is further defined by a number of functions. Table 9.1 provides an overview of these dimensions and their related functions.

Table 9.1   The Building Material of School Improvement

1. **Vision for Learning**
   A. Developing vision
   B. Articulating vision
   C. Implementing vision
   D. Stewarding vision

2. **Instructional Program**
   A. Knowledge and involvement
   B. Hiring and allocating staff
   C. Supporting staff
   D. Instructional time

3. **Curricular Program**
   A. Knowledge and involvement
   B. Expectations, standards
   C. Opportunity to learn
   D. Curriculum alignment

4. **Assessment Program**
   A. Knowledge and involvement
   B. Assessment procedures
   C. Monitoring instruction and curriculum
   D. Communication and use of data

Vision for Learning

Leaders in high-performing schools devote considerable energy to "the development, articulation, implementation, and stewardship of a vision of learning that is shared and supported by the school community" (Interstate School Leaders Consortium, 1996, p. 10). On the development end of the continuum, leaders ensure that the vision and mission of the school are crafted with and among stakeholders. They also ensure that a variety of sources of data that illuminate student learning are used in the forging of vision and goals. In particular, they make certain that (1) assessment data related to student learning, (2) demographic data pertaining to students and the community, and (3) information on patterns of opportunity to learn are featured in the development process.

Effective leaders facilitate the creation of a school vision that reflects high and appropriate standards of learning, a belief in the educability of all students, and high levels of personal and organizational performance. They emphasize ambitious goals, ones that call for improvement over the status

Go to **www.learningsciences.com/bookresources** to download figures and tables.

quo. In particular, leadership for school improvement means making certain that goals are focused on students, feature student learning and achievement, and are clearly defined. Instructionally anchored leaders ensure that responsibility for achieving targets is made explicit and that timelines for achieving objectives are specified. In short, they make sure that the school vision is translated into specific and measurable end results. They also ensure that the resources needed to meet goals are clearly identified—and made available to the school community.

Effective principals and other school-based leaders articulate the vision through personal modeling and by communicating with others in and around the organization. On the first front, they are adept at making the school vision central to their own daily work. They demonstrate through their action the organization's commitment to the values and beliefs at the heart of the mission as well as to the specific activities needed to reach goals. On the second issue, communication, school improvement–oriented leaders work ceaselessly to promote the school's mission and agenda to staff, students, parents, and members of the extended school community (e.g., business and religious leaders, district office staff). Indeed, effective leaders are masters in keeping vision, mission, and goals in the forefront of everyone's attention and at the center of everyone's work. To accomplish this, they engage a wide array of formal and informal avenues of exchange and employ a variety of techniques (e.g., symbols, ceremonies).

Master leaders are especially well versed at translating vision into operation and at stewarding the school's vision. They are careful monitors, (1) ensuring a continuous examination of assumptions, beliefs, and values; (2) assessing implementation of goals; and (3) evaluating the impact of school objectives on organizational performance and student learning. One way these leaders shepherd goals is through the actions they take to recognize, celebrate, and reward the contributions of community members to the development, implementation, and, most important, realization of school goals. At the same time, they do not overlook shortcoming and failures. Certainly a critical dimension of operationalizing and stewarding is seeing to it that school vision and school goals shape routine school activities and anchor organizational systems and structures. On a personal front, operationalizing and shepherding occurs when leaders act as keepers and promoters of the vision; maintain enthusiasm and a sense of optimism, especially in periods of waning energy; and inspire others to break through barriers to make the school vision a reality.

Instructional Program

Leaders in highly productive schools have a strong orientation to and affinity for the core technology of their business—learning and teaching. In the area of pedagogy, they are knowledgeable about and deeply involved in the instructional program of the school and are heavily invested in instruction, spending considerable time on the teaching function. They model the importance of teaching by being directly involved in the design and implementation of the instructional program. They pay attention to teaching, visiting classrooms and working with groups of teachers on instructional issues, in both formal and informal settings.

Leaders in schools where all youngsters reach ambitious learning targets realize that teachers are the keystones of a quality education. Therefore, they devote considerable time and undertake much careful planning to guarantee that the school is populated with excellent teachers and with colleagues whose values and instructional frameworks are consistent with the mission and culture of the school. Instructionally centered leaders are also diligent in assigning teachers to various responsibilities. They allocate teachers based on educational criteria, especially student needs, rather than on less appropriate foundations such as staff seniority and school politics.

We see again and again throughout the research that instructionally grounded leaders devote abundant time to supporting colleagues in their efforts to strengthen teaching and learning in and across classrooms. Foremost, they are aggressive in identifying and removing barriers that prevent colleagues from doing their work well. They provide intellectual stimulation and make certain that teachers have a high-quality stream of job-embedded opportunities to expand, enhance, and refine their repertoires of instructional skills. They also make sure that the materials that teachers require to perform their jobs are on hand in sufficient quantity and in a timely fashion. Consistent with the involvement and investment theme, effective leaders demonstrate personal interest in staff and make themselves available to them.

We know from the literature that feedback on performance is essential to the learning process, and leaders in high-performing schools are diligent about providing this information to colleagues on a consistent basis and in a timely manner. In supplying performance feedback, learning-centered leaders (1) rely on personal knowledge developed through numerous classroom observations, both informal and formal, and (2) employ a variety of supervisory and evaluation strategies. They make student learning the calculus of the exchange process. Effective leaders are especially expert in opening up a wide assortment of improvement opportunities for teachers. And they are relentless in counseling poor teachers to leave the classroom. In a related vein, improvement-focused leaders aggressively monitor the instructional program in its entirety, ensuring alignment between learning standards and objectives and classroom instruction.

Academic learning time is the caldron in which student achievement materializes and effective leaders work tirelessly with staff to ensure that this precious resource is maximized. They begin by making sure that the great bulk of time is devoted to instructional activities and that noninstructional time is kept to a minimum. They also see to it that the majority of instructional time is dedicated to core academic subjects. Within this learning space, they work with teachers to accentuate the use of instructional strategies that maximize student engagement at high levels of success. On a parallel track, improvement-focused leaders undertake an array of activities that protect valuable instructional time from interruptions, including (1) assigning academic subjects time slots that are least likely to be disturbed by school events; (2) protecting teachers from distractions from the school office; (3) developing, implementing, and monitoring procedures to reduce student tardiness and absenteeism; and (4) ensuring that teachers are punctual. They also foster more productive use of time by coordinating time usage among teachers and across classes (e.g., all language arts instruction unfolding during the first two hours of the day).

Finally, leaders in high-performing schools are expert in providing recognition and rewards for quality teaching and demonstrated student learning. They systematically celebrate the instructional accomplishments of the school and recognize and reward individual achievement. They employ both public avenues of acknowledgment and private praise and encouragement to colleagues. They link recognition, incentives, and rewards.

Curriculum Program

School improvement–centered leaders are also knowledgeable about and deeply involved in the school's curricular program. They work with colleagues to ensure that the school is defined by a rigorous curricular program in general and that each student's program in particular is of high quality. On the first issue, they establish high standards and expectations in the various curricular domains consistent with blueprints crafted by professional associations and learned societies. On the second topic, they ensure that the opportunity to learn is maximized for each youngster. These leaders are also diligent in monitoring and evaluating the effectiveness of the school's curricular program.

In the array of factors that define high-performing schools, curriculum alignment enjoys a position of prominence, and effective leaders are especially attentive to creating a "tightly coupled curriculum" throughout the school. This means they ensure that objectives (standards), instruction, curriculum materials, and assessments are all carefully coordinated. It also means that all special programs (e.g., bilingual education) are brought into the gravitational field of the regular program. Finally, it means that there is a high degree of coordination (1) across subjects within grades, (2) across grade levels and phases of schooling (e.g., from the elementary to the middle school), and (3) among teachers within and across departments and grade levels.

Assessment Program

As we saw with the instructional and curricular programs, school improvement–focused leaders are knowledgeable about assessment practices and personally involved with colleagues in crafting, implementing, and monitoring assessment systems at the classroom and school levels. They provide resources—time, funding, and materials—to bring well-developed assessment systems to life. Through personal modeling, they promote a serious attitude toward data-based decision making among their colleagues.

Assessment systems in schools with effective leaders are characterized by a variety of distinguishing elements. First, they are comprehensive. They address classroom and school-based activity. They feature the use of a wide variety of monitoring and data-collection strategies, both formal and informal. That is, they ensure that student learning is measured using an assortment of techniques. For example, comprehensive designs often include teacher record-keeping systems, end-of-level or end-of-unit reports, student work products, criterion-referenced tests, and standardized measures of student performance. They also highlight information gleaned from direct observations in classrooms. Second, they disaggregate information on the important conditions and outcomes of schooling (e.g., program placement of students, test results) by relevant biosocial characteristics of students (e.g., gender, race, class). Third, they are constructed in ways that foster the triangulation of data from multiple sources in arriving at judgments concerning the effectiveness of curriculum and instructional programs and organizational operations. Finally, as alluded to previously, these systems highlight tight alignment between classroom-based and school-based methods of assessing student learning.

We close here where we began. In schools with effective assessment programs, the fingerprints of school leaders are distinctly visible. The literature informs us that effective leaders are master craftspersons in the communication and use of the data that form the lifeblood of the assessment system. On the issue of use, improvement-grounded leaders ensure that assessment data are at the heart of (1) mission development, (2) instructional planning, (3) the evaluation of the curricular program, (4) the identification and design of services for special needs students, (5) monitoring progress on school goals and improvement efforts, and (6) the evaluation of school staff. On the communication front, instructionally based leaders provide teachers and parents with assessment results on a regular basis. They also unpack the meaning of results with staff—as a body of the whole, in appropriate groups, and individually. They make certain that information on student progress is regularly reported to students and parents in an accessible form, at multiple times, across an array of forums, and in multiple formats.

Chapter 10

The Norms of School as Academic Place

In this chapter, we investigate how leaders can help create a climate of instructional press in schools. The focus is on forging and nurturing broad norms of schools as academic places: academic care, challenge, task-focused goals, actively guided learning, engagement and vitality, cooperative work, meaningfulness, student-anchored learning, and evidence-based action and feedback.

Academic Care

Across the landscape of work on productive classrooms and effective schools, we find that educators employ caring relationships with students to foster the development of powerful academic norms. Effective teachers harness relationships in the service of academic achievement. Students describe good teachers as those who care about them and make them learn. They often describe caring student–teacher relationships as academic in nature. Academic care becomes a blend of personalized support and press for academic mastery.

Students explain the norm of academic care in a variety of ways. They describe teachers who do not let them fall through the cracks or become invisible. They discuss teachers who push and pull them to understanding and success. In places where the norms of academic care flourish, teachers cajole, nudge, and command students to complete assignments. They are alert, approachable, and helpful. They build safety nets to ensure success. Teachers ensure that every child receives the needed academic support. They work hard to prevent failure, employing a variety of academic care strategies to ensure this outcome.

Challenge

Academic challenge characterizes effective classrooms and schools. Evidence from an assortment of studies and reviews affirms the centrality of the norm of challenge in the learning narrative and its influence on critical outcomes. For example, Yair (2000, p. 501) documents that "the odds of students engaging in their lessons in what they named 'most challenging' are 90% higher than the odds in the lessons students identify as 'least challenging.'" The conclusion is clear: when students report challenge, they also demonstrate engagement.

Unfortunately, as is the case for all of the norms of academic place, challenge is often underdeveloped in schools. As analysts have documented, engagement is often conspicuous by its absence in schools. We add here that some part of this lack of engagement is traceable to a lack of challenge in classrooms, especially in terms of expectations and assignments. We confirm also that schools and classrooms often reinforce rather than disrupt the expectations and demands students carry with them from interactions in other societal institutions. Researchers also convey the importance of context and nuance around the norm of challenge. To begin with, it is not a fixed quality. It can be understood only in reference to students. By definition, challenge is always a moving target, increasing as the skills and knowledge of the learners are strengthened. Therefore, the critical issue is challenging youngsters at the correct level.

Task-Focused Goals

Scholars over the last thirty years have uncovered the significance of a specific dimension of challenge—goals—to the development of classrooms and schools as academic places. According to Hattie (2009, p. 199), "setting challenging goals is a powerful part of the overall equation of what makes the difference in learning." Of particular interest here is the difference in emphasis on task-oriented goals (also known as mastery goals) versus performance-oriented goals. Task-oriented goals address establishing expectations to achievement targets. Performance-oriented goals focus on comparisons of student learning outcomes. Task-oriented goals foreground effort. Performance-oriented goals underscore ability.

Task-oriented goals are characterized by (1) clarity in the specifics of the learning intentions (i.e., they provide directionable guidance to staff and students) and (2) difficulty and specificity. As was the case with challenge in general, challenging goals are most effective when they exist in the company of the other norms of the school as academic place. For example, challenging goals work best when they are (1) coupled with varied and meaningful learning opportunities, (2) feature structured and attainable targets, (3) provide large doses of feedback from teachers, (4) make success clear and visible in comparison to mastery rather than to the performance of other children, (5) underscore problem-anchored activities, and (6) highlight collaborative efforts.

As is the case with each of the norms of academic place, we know that task-focused goals lead to important outcomes. They promote greater effort on the part of students and deep persistence with assignments; ramp up engagement; and increase student learning. For example, in his cardinal analysis Hattie (2009, p. 164) concludes that "the performance of students who have the most challenging goals is over 250 percent higher than the performance of the subjects with easiest goals."

Actively Guided Learning

From a large cache of research, we know that (1) teachers occupy center stage in classes for the overwhelming bulk of the day, something in the neighborhood of 80 percent of time; (2) lecture and discussion is the disproportionately preferred method of teaching; (3) about one-third of the time teachers are teaching what students already know; and (4) students are engaged in their classes, on the average, no more than 50 percent of available class time. For a significant part of the school day, teachers and students are involved in the learning process in only a ritualistic fashion. The sequela is hardly surprising. Neither extrinsic nor intrinsic motivation develops. Effort is withheld. Students learn considerably less than they are capable of and less than what would be helpful to them to be successful in school and beyond.

Schools as academic places, on the other hand, are characterized as venues of active learning. Unlike traditional schools, they privilege learning over teaching. The focus is less about the transmission of knowledge and more about the construction of understanding. It is less about individualism and more about collaboration. The framework of school as academic place is about pulling students into their own learning. In actively guided learning, teachers are unquestionably authoritative directors of action, not merely facilitators, but not authoritarian. They are less about telling and presenting academic work than requiring children to be active initiators of their own learning under the guidance of academically caring adults. Academic places are defined by student commitment, involvement, and efficacy. Given the reality that involvement precedes learning, we should not be surprised to learn that active, guided learning has been consistently found to be linked to student autonomy, self-regulation, and achievement. And as we reported with the other norms, active learning works best in the portfolio of norms of academic place than as a singular characteristic.

Engagement and Vitality

Schools as academic places are venues of participation and engagement, not passivity, ritual, and boredom. Researchers and practitioners provide useful details in the narrative on student engagement. We know from the previous discussion that schools as academic places are both student centered and teacher directed. Students in engaging classrooms have voice and choice. They are in places where construction trumps transmission. Thus the norm of engagement underscores project-based learning opportunities and application-oriented tasks, as well as work that is interesting, varied, and meaningful. In engaging classrooms, or when the norm of engagement and vitality is present, one is likely to find cooperative and student-directed learning experiences.

As we have reported on the other norms of schools as academic places, measurable benefits flow to schools from the norm of engagement and vitality, benefits such as improved attitudes toward subject domains, augmentation in critical thinking skills, positive affect, and enhanced achievement. Engagement in school as academic place is described by Csikszentmihalyi and Larson (1984) as "flow," "a state of deep involvement in which the clock is figuratively turned off, where there is a loss of consciousness" (p. 250). Active, guided, engaged learning brings inspiration and vitality to the school in general and the teaching–learning process in particular. Academic place is about energy, excitement, and meaningfulness.

Cooperative Work

We begin with a perhaps obvious but essential reminder. That is, the norms of school as academic place are interlocking and share a good deal of space. The more of them that materialize in robust ways, the better things are for school improvement and student learning. So far we have examined five of these norms: academic care, challenge, task-focused goals, actively guided learning, and engagement and vitality. Here we turn to the sixth norm, cooperative work. This norm is also described in terms of collaboration, inclusion, and integration. Collaborative work challenges a number of underpinnings of traditional classrooms. It pushes back on the belief in imparted wisdom, the nearly exclusive centrality of the transmission of knowledge, the authoritarian aspects of the classroom. It also underscores the importance of task completion, rolling back a primary focus on the competitive aspects of the classroom. We also see that the academic norms of community-focused learning push the notion that learning is predominantly an individual activity from center stage. Collaborative learning requires that students attend to task-focused and challenging goals to accomplish meaningful work. The essential element here is that children are responsible for their learning and that of their peers. There is a palpable sense of interdependency in classrooms.

Analysis of collaboration spotlights the importance of the topic of peers in classrooms, with eyes focused directly on teaching. We begin with the reminder that students have a tremendous say about what they do or do not learn. We layer in the reality that peer work runs against the ingrained norms in learning and teaching, such as learning is an individual pursuit, competition is the appropriate framework for learning, and learning occurs primarily through transmission. Not surprisingly then, collaboration is not part of the fabric of most schools.

The empirical scorecard on the value of the norm of collaboration is quite positive in general and particularly robust for groups of students who often do not flourish in schools—minority students and working-class youngsters. Researchers also substantiate that engagement is an outcome of peer work and that learning benefits accrue to youngsters who work in a collaborative environment in general and in models of peer tutoring in particular.

Meaningfulness

There is a considerable body of knowledge that reveals that schools as academic places are defined by meaningful work and authentic pedagogy. The norm of meaningfulness assumes a variety of forms in the literature, or more accurately perhaps is an amalgam of varied but highly related ideas. In its essence, it boils down to work in which youngsters are apt to engage. One dimension of this is the authenticity of the work, its purposefulness (i.e., infusing activities with purpose and signaling that work is important). Meaningfulness also includes the element of responsiveness, the idea that schools are classrooms adapted to the specific needs and interests of the students. The artificial barrier between school and the world outside of schooling is lowered. When the norm of meaningfulness is present, there is a heavy concentration on performance tasks and problem-based activities. Multiple and varied ways exist for students to demonstrate understanding and to be able to do so in ways that have value to students and to those outside the confines of the learning assignment.

We also see in classes defined by the norm of meaningfulness that there is a strong strand of application of knowledge that supplements the development of knowledge. Work is marked by concreteness as well as abstraction. The significance of relevance is underscored here. Culturally relevant and culturally congruent activities are visible where the norm of meaningfulness is found. The essential idea is culturally responsive pedagogy and curriculum. We also find a focus on work and outcomes valued by students and consequently attention to having students assume responsibility for their efforts. When the norm of meaningfulness is present, group accountability and rewards supplement traditional, individual-based accountability. Meaningful instruction has a powerful pull on student engagement. Indeed, as Yair (2000, p. 501) concludes, "the odds of students engaging in the classes they deem 'most relevant' are 108% higher than in the classes the students dubbed the 'least relevant.'" And research consistently has shown that engagement is the gateway to learning.

Student-Anchored Learning

The eighth norm of school as academic place is student-grounded work, a principle with a great deal of alignment with the earlier norms. At its core, it underscores students as powerful activists in their learning. At the macro level, this means educators seeing schools and learning through the eyes of their students, not simply through the demands of the curriculum and the needs of the school as an institution. We find here, for example, building instruction around the experiences of the learners. We see this as making schools and schoolwork relevant to students, fitting classroom work to the larger world outside of schooling, and emphasizing real-life applications. The norm of student-anchored work also includes teaching and learning in which student choice and voice receive considerable attention, frames that, in turn, are linked to student commitment, engagement, and learning.

Evidence-Based Action and Feedback

Schools as academic places are distinguished by the attention given to evidence in decision-making processes. There has been a great deal of attention devoted to data-based decision making over the last quarter century. This is appropriate. Data-based decision making, however, is often limited in important ways. It has generally been held that data are academic scores of one kind or another. More limiting still has been the restriction of data to standardized assessments. Most troubling has been the impoverished conceptions of monitoring and feedback in data-based decision making. A broader perspective highlights evidence for nearly all actions undertaken in schools and underscores the essential element of feedback.

In effective schools, evidence becomes a central plank in dialogue and decision making through the school and across the full spectrum of activities. Schools as academic places are venues marked by a generalizable narrative of inquiry and action on the academic and social learning of students. In schools as academic places, considerable thought is given to the explicit cause–effect linkages between instructional actions and student learning. At the heart of evidence-based action is the principle of feedback. We see the key ingredients of helpful feedback in the research. Productive feedback is focused on the level where students are working. It is directed to progress on tasks and the processes embedded in those tasks rather than to the self at a personal level. It is generally positive in form, and it offers understanding from correct rather than incorrect answers.

Looking across the norms that define schools as academic places, we see the presence of three deeply entwined principles. First, these are places where learning has priority over teaching, where students are active parties of the schoolwork and producers, not simply receivers, of learning. Second, excellent instruction is defined primarily on both the process and content of teaching. Third, these are places of academic community.

Chapter 11

Leadership for Learning: Culture and Community

In this chapter, we turn the analysis to leading the cultural dimension of schools. We focus on communities of learning, organizational culture, and communities of care for students (see Table 11.1).

Table 11.1 Learning-Centered Leadership: Leading School Culture and Community

1. Communities of Learning A. Professional development B. Communities of professional practice C. Community-anchored schools
2. Organizational Culture A. Production emphasis B. Continuous improvement C. Orderly learning environment D. Personalized environment
3. Communities of Care A. Ethics B. Stakeholder engagement

Communities of Learning

Effective school leaders are especially skillful in creating learning organizations fostering the development of communities of learning. They are vigorous promoters of professional development, they nurture the growth of communities of professional practice, and they shape school organizations to adhere to the principles of community.

In the area of staff development, improvement-focused leaders thoughtfully attend to their own growth, modeling a lifelong commitment to learning for their colleagues. Unlike many peers, these women and men focus their learning on issues of school improvement. And they assume an active role in planning and evaluating specific staff learning activities and the overall professional development system of the school. Attending to professional development is a significant piece of their work portfolios.

In working with colleagues, instructionally centered leaders establish an expectation that the continual expansion of one's knowledge and skills focused on helping students succeed is the norm at the school. These leaders also demonstrate a dedication and a willingness to assist teachers in strengthening their instructional skills. They furnish needed resources to teachers, including support to help teachers gain new knowledge (e.g., they fund workshops, hire coaches, facilitate intra- and inter-school visitations), and they provide the materials teachers require to implement new skills in the classroom. These leaders are committed to ensuring that their colleagues have both direct and indirect, both formal and informal guidance as they work to integrate skills learned during professional development into their portfolios of instructional behaviors. They are well versed in providing regular "incidental interventions"—casual conversations and suggestions of ideas—that assist teachers in their efforts to improve instruction. And, as I outline in the following text, they create systems and procedures that nurture this type of informal learning throughout the school, mechanisms that promote the exchange of professional dialogue about strengthening instruction and improving the school.

Improvement-centered leaders forge a structure for professional development from the principles of learning theory and models of best practice. They make certain that a robust system for developing staff expertise is in place and that members have the learning experiences necessary to grow their instructional skills. They ensure that development opportunities and experiences flow from data on student achievement, link carefully with district and school goals, are integrated into the culture of the school, and focus on student learning. These leaders also make sure that learning activities are scaffolded on the principles of adult learning and the best professional development standards.

Leaders of schools on the crest of the improvement curve actively promote the formation of a learning organization, the development of staff cohesion and support, and the growth of communities of professional practice. At the broadest level, these leaders endeavor to create a culture of collaboration and the systems, operations, and policies that provide the infrastructure for that collegial culture. At this level, they also are active in building shared beliefs concerning the importance of community. They nurture collaborative processes (e.g., share decision making), forge schedules (e.g., common planning time), and create organizational structures (e.g., team leadership) that permit and encourage shared mission and direction, collaborative work, and mutual accountability for school goals and student learning. These leaders are particularly attentive to ensuring that there are a variety of mechanisms for teachers to communicate and work among themselves. And, to be sure, these women and men are active participants in the various school learning communities, often serving key linking and pollinating roles in the process. They understand, and help others understand, that communities of professional practice offer the most appropriate vessels for professional learning and the forging of new instructional skills. Finally, they take advantage of the fact that they are in a unique position to garner and allocate resources to bring communities of professional practice to life.

As we saw in Part 2, school organizations in the twentieth century featured the principles of hierarchy (e.g., line authority, impersonality, the separation of management from labor, the specialization and division of work, and so forth). Over the years, we have learned that more effective schools underscore the principles of community (e.g., authority based on expertise, personalization, shared leadership, overlapping work, and so forth). There is considerable evidence that leadership is the key factor in rebuilding and reculturing schools in the form of communities.

Through their actions, leaders both communicate the importance of community in a school and reveal the meaning of this core idea to students, staff, and parents. At the broadest and most comprehensive level, they accomplish this by demonstrating an ethic of care throughout the school. More concretely, they treat all individuals with fairness, dignity, and respect. In the process of doing all this, these leaders form the glue that holds the community together (i.e., trust) and build the foundations that support the three key pillars of community—shared direction, cooperative work, and mutual accountability.

Improvement-oriented leaders are master craftspersons in the formation and use of group processes, both in their own work and in the school community writ large. These leaders model effective skills in the areas of (1) problem framing and problem solving, (2) decision making, (3) conflict resolution, (4) consensus building, and (5) communication. They also see to it that these important processes permeate the organization.

Leaders in high-performing schools also often promote a shared or team approach to leading the organization. The DNA of this more distributed conception of management—of pushing leadership outward to students, parents, and especially staff and helping others assume the mantle of leadership—is the privileging of expertise, rather than role, in managing the school. Effective leaders are adept in meeting this challenge. They involve others in the crafting and implementation of important decisions. They empower others and provide faculty with voice—both formal and informal—in running the school, not simply their own classrooms. They delegate often and effectively and frequently form leadership teams to assist in shaping the vision and in managing the operations of the school, especially in and around the core technology.

Organizational Culture

Patterns in the tapestry of organizational culture are clearly visible in the material examined to this point. For example, the research on communities of learning illuminates a number of themes that help define organizational culture (e.g., shared work). Here we augment our understanding of culture by introducing four new themes: production emphasis, continuous improvement, safe and orderly learning environment, and personalized community.

Effective organizations in all sectors, including education, are marked by a strong production focus. Consistent with the core theme of our review, improvement-focused leadership is a key factor in explaining the presence of this organizational orientation toward outcomes. On the front end of this condition, leaders in high-performing schools work ceaselessly to create an environment of high performance expectations for self, staff, and students. On a personal front, they model performance expectations. They model risk taking in the service of attaining important goals. They regularly communicate a concern for and interest in staff performance and student achievement. They establish clearly defined, schoolwide academic standards to bring high expectations to life. They carefully ensure that these high expectations are translated into school policies (e.g., all students must take Algebra I by the end of the ninth grade, work below the grade of "C" must be redone) and behavioral expectations (e.g., homework in this school is completed on time). These leaders make certain that expectations are decoupled from beliefs about biological and social characteristics of students (e.g., the belief that second-language learners require remedial work in all subject areas).

On the backside of production emphasis, effective leaders regularly assess the results of school practices and examine their impact on student success and maintain school accountability. They hold everyone—students, teachers, parents, and school administrators—responsible for achieving school goals and reaching targets in the area of student performance, providing special weight to the contributions of teachers and other professional staff at the school. While these leaders acknowledge the value of hard work, they clearly couple success to performance.

Instructionally grounded leaders are the catalysts in school-based efforts at continuous improvement. They understand and communicate that complacency is the enemy of improvement, that the status quo is more tightly linked to decline than to growth. These leaders confront stagnation. They ensure that the school systematically reviews and adopts more productive strategies to accomplish important goals. They take risks and encourage others to do so in the quest for better education. They act entrepreneurially to support school improvement efforts. They encourage initiative and proactiveness. They make sure that the assessment program is a driver in the work of continuous school improvement.

From the earliest studies of effective schools, we have known that schools in which all youngsters reach ambitious targets of performance are defined by safe and orderly learning environments. In terms of the physical facilities, this means that the school plant, equipment, and support systems operate safely, efficiently, and effectively. It also means that a safe, clean, and aesthetically pleasing school environment is created and maintained. Finally, it means that problems with facilities are identified, addressed, and resolved in a timely manner.

As with many of the areas we explore in this review, leaders have a dual role in the domain of learning environment. On the one hand, they demonstrate what is valued through their own behaviors. Thus, effective leaders model appropriate behavior by personally enforcing discipline with students and by confronting problems quickly and forcefully. On the other hand, these leaders are responsible for the creation and operation of systems and structures and the performance of colleagues. In this area, they ensure that operations, rules, and procedures to maintain discipline and order in the school community are developed and monitored on a regular basis. Specifically, they make certain that classroom and school rules and consequences are clearly defined, communicated, and understood by students, teachers, and parents. In the process, they work to secure widespread acceptance and support for the school code of conduct. Effective school leaders are masterful at involving members of the school community in the development of the school's discipline processes. They work hard to ensure that school rules are fairly and consistently enforced across the school community. They provide assistance to individual teachers and support for the management system itself. Perhaps most critically, they demand collective accountability for student behavior.

There is a fair amount of research that shows that impersonality reigns in many schools in America, especially secondary schools. That is, students are neither well known nor particularly well cared for. Since, as we have seen, schools have been constructed using institutional and hierarchical blueprints, both of which feature impersonality, this condition should come as a surprise to no one. Yet the fact that it can be explained is not much consolation to the youngsters in these schools. On the other side of the ledger, we know that in schools where academic and social learning thrive, high academic press is almost always coupled with high personalization. At the broadest level, this indicates that each student is well known and cared for, and that each youngster feels valued and important at school.

Effective leaders address personalization by forging structures and mechanisms for students to form ties to the school and to appropriate adult role models (e.g., the use of teacher advisors and the structures to support the advisory process), by creating multiple opportunities for meaningful student engagement. They work to link students and teachers in a variety of school-level activities. Leadership for school improvement means nurturing personalization by (1) creating opportunities for students to exercise responsibility and to practice leadership behaviors (i.e., to assume important roles in the school community), (2) offering chances for students to develop the skills needed to assume leadership roles, and (3) crafting programs that acknowledge and reward participation. Effective leaders also understand the significance of symbols. They are expert at fostering the widespread use of school symbols that distinguish the school from the larger community and that clearly characterize students as members of the school.

Recognition and rewards also fill a central cell in the personalization design in high-performing schools. In these communities, an abundance of classroom-based and schoolwide recognition systems and mechanisms are in play, systems that are carefully designed to be reinforcing. Rewards are distributed frequently, and they reach a high percentage of students. They are seen as meaningful and important throughout the school community, especially to students. They are often public in nature. They highlight the accomplishments of individuals and groups. And while they unquestionably privilege academic accomplishments, rewards are provided for success in a wide array of areas. We close our narrative here with an important reminder. Leadership is the central ingredient in ensuring that these frameworks of meaningful student engagement and widespread rewards and recognition become defining elements of school culture.

Communities of Care for Students

The explanatory narrative begins with this essential reality: "It is students themselves, in the end, not teachers, who decide what students will learn" (Hattie, 2009, p. 241), and students do not volunteer effort when they are detached from school. Schooling for students is profoundly voluntary. Children have to "go to school." The decision to "do schooling" is substantially their own. This means, of course, that they are key decision makers in the learning production. The major purpose of a supportive learning community is to positively influence students' willingness to learn what the school believes they require to be successful in life, to cause students to embrace academic challenges, and to help them reach those ends.

Educators in general and leaders in particular have three options at this point: ignore this reality, fight to change it, or use it as a platform for action. The first and second options have been the tools of choice for education historically. This is hardly surprising given the institutional nature of schooling and the managerial logic of school leadership we outlined earlier. The problem is, however, that these choices have not been especially effective, especially for students placed in peril by society and schooling. Supportive learning communities for students move the profession to option three, weaving the wisdom, needs, concerns, interests, and worries of students deeply into the "doing of schooling" without sacrificing academic press. Or more globally, it requires educators to acknowledge that achieving valued outcomes for students occurs within school cultures. For example, research confirms that social concerns form the caldron of interest for students in schools. It also shows us that to reach working-class youngsters we need to address social connections beyond the schoolhouse. The charge for school leaders is to work these and related realities productively in the service of helping students master essential academic goals.

On the research front, a deep line of empirical findings concludes that school communities in which many young persons find themselves, especially older students and youngsters in peril, do not exert the positive influence and support necessary for them to commit to "do schooling." While this is not the place to examine this line of analysis in detail, we need to point out that student disengagement, often passive, sometimes active, is common in schools. This is hardly surprising given that one of the pillars of institutions and bureaucracy is impersonality. As Ancess (2003, p. 83) reminds us, because of this "schools are conventionally organized as though relationships are not only unimportant and irrelevant, but an obstacle to efficient operation."

Analysts have uncovered a good deal of knowledge about what supportive communities of pastoral care for students look like and how they function. A supportive learning community is defined by essential norms (care, support, safety, and membership). These norms combine to produce intermediate outcomes, such as student learning dispositions and psychological states, that in turn lead to academic engagement. All of this powers student learning.

Communities of pastoral care emphasize two strategies: one working to overcome liabilities and the other to build up assets. To begin with then, communities of pastoral care protect young persons from harmful conditions. They suppress factors that undermine hopes for success, such as the formation of dysfunctional and oppositional peer cultures. Personalization damps down aspects of schooling that push students away from engaging the work of "doing school" well. A supportive learning community provides protective power while attacking social problems that place students in peril. It helps create an environment that neutralizes home and community problems and individual characteristics that foster social marginalization and academic disengagement.

Concomitantly, scholars document that supportive learning environments create assets, social and human capital, to draw youngsters into the hard work that is required to be successful in school. They transform schools into places where the culture promotes commitment to learning. Assets such as care and warmth are stockpiled to assist in helping students reach ambitious learning targets.

According to the literature, effective leaders act with integrity, fairness, and in an ethical manner. On one front, this means that leaders fulfill legal and contractual obligations and apply laws and district and school policies and procedures fairly, wisely, and considerately. It means that they guarantee the privacy rights of students and recognize and respect the legitimate authority of others. At a deeper level, it means that leaders treat others fairly, equitably, and with dignity and respect—and they establish the expectation that others in the school community act in a similar manner.

On a personal basis, effective leaders are more cognizant than their peers of their own values and beliefs, and they shape their behavior in accord with personal and professional codes of ethics. They are more reflective and self-critical regarding their own practice and its impact on others in the extended school community. They know the difference between using office and position for one's own gain and for the benefit of the school community, and they honor the latter. These leaders serve as role models in terms of accepting responsibility for what happens to children and families in their school community.

Finally, the research on high-performing schools and improvement-oriented leaders reveals that effective leaders are attuned to and expert at linking the school to parents and others in the extended school community. Much more so than peers, these leaders weigh connections in terms of their value in enhancing the academic and social learning of students. That is, they engage families and other community members in the service of school goals, the learning agenda, and student performance. Inside the school, these women and men model community collaboration for staff, establish norms regarding the importance of parent connections, and provide opportunities for staff to develop the collaborative skills needed to work effectively with parents. They also ensure that information on family and community concerns, expectations, and interests inform school decisions.

Leadership for school improvement means working from a comprehensive design in respect of school–community relations that is anchored by the school's academic mission. The plan is systematic, not simply a collection of ad hoc and unrelated activities. In the wider community, effective leaders develop relationships with influential actors in the religious, business, and political sectors. They are actively involved in the school community and communicate frequently with stakeholders therein. They employ multiple channels and a variety of forums to operationalize these connections. Their objectives are to inform, promote, learn, and link—to ensure that the school and the community serve one another as resources. On the extended community front, effective leaders are also especially attentive to building bridges with (1) other youth and family service agencies that can promote better lives for youngsters and their families and (2) the media that can help promote the image of the school.

For improvement-centered leaders, connections with parents occupy a strategic position in the algorithm of stakeholder engagement. Leaders communicate with families regularly and through a variety of channels. They create programs and strategies that bring parents from the periphery to the inner circle of school operations. In particular, they foster the development of parent education programs, including activities that (1) encourage and help parents learn about the instructional and curricular program at the school, (2) assist parents in working more productively with their children at home on the goals of the school, and (3) assist parents in extending their own parenting skills.

Chapter 12

The Caring Leader

(with Mark Smylie and Karen Seashore Louis)

What to Care About in the Work on Caring

Over the last dozen years in investigating the world of school improvement, we have arrived at the following premise: caring is a core pillar in improvement work. We know that less care equates with lowered odds of students performing well in school in terms of academic and social learning. A scarcity of care is particularly hazardous to youngsters placed at peril by society and its institutions. Thus, care in schools is essential. We also consistently find that teachers and principals are caring people. They care about their students and they care for them.

At the same time, we see forces in play that at a minimum do not support the development and nurturing of caring and at worse provide a toxic environment for care to take root and grow in schools. One basket of these forces emanates from the economic, political, and social environment in which schools conduct their work. To begin with, as Rauner (2000, p. 130) explains, "the idea of caring has been privatized and thus has been made irrelevant to the public sphere." She goes on to note that "as the habits of interaction that characterize care have been made to seem appropriate only in the private sphere . . . care no longer has a voice in discussions of how we act as workers, or what we expect of our peers or leaders." This devaluing of care in society provides an impoverished framework for building caring schools in general and nurturing caring leadership in particular.

Almost all of the external pressure on schools directs educators to focus on "academic press"; that is, to push and pull children to success via the instructional program, increasingly at the cost of relational care. While academic press is one of two core pillars of school success, it represents only half the framework. The concern today, as educators regularly tell us, is that academic press has been consistently pushed onto schools as the only hope for children. We know that both press and care are required to create schools that work well for all children. We also know that their power is significantly amplified when they are employed in tandem in an interlocking manner.

Other forces from within the schoolhouse also push the spotlight away from care. Paradoxically, one of those dynamics is the "assumption of care" in schools. When we ask teachers and formal school leaders if they and the school care about their young charges, we receive a 100 percent positive response. However, when we ask these three follow-up questions, very few hands are raised: (1) You have the core aspects of your academic program well established (i.e., language, mathematics, science, and so forth). What are the analog elements that the school has identified and to which you pay attention on the caring side of the equation? (2) What strategies have you settled on to bring each of the elements of care to life? And (3), if we come to your school on March 22 and ask to see how Tammy Jeffries is doing in the core domains of the academic program, you would show us a good deal of evidence. What evidence will you provide to show that Tammy is cared for at Burnett Middle School when we visit? Since there is considerable evidence that measurement focuses attention, this is a troubling reality.

In addition, there is little attention in schools to how caring works. We know, for example, that caring is indirect in its influence. Care can lead to important conditions (e.g., enhanced self-esteem, stronger motivation), conditions that can help us to discern how well caring is working. But absent knowledge of what those conditions are, teachers and principals are handicapped in their efforts to forge and assess care.

Three final issues need attention in our quest to answer the question of "what to care about in the work on caring." First, caring in the educational literature is universally seen as a means to a more valuable end. It needs to be acknowledged that caring can be an instrumental act. At the same time, it is important to acknowledge that care is a worthy end in itself. It is why youth-serving organizations such as schools exist. Second, the topic of care in schools is almost always a matter of care for students. The focus is good; the exclusivity is not. In schools, care works best when it cascades across everyone. This means that a good deal more interest needs to be devoted to the care of teachers and parents than is currently the case. The waves of depersonalization of teachers and the mechanization of teaching over the last quarter century have come at a steep cost. In short, it is difficult to be a giver of care in a group when one feels uncared for oneself. Finally, and related to the previous analysis, the idea of caring organizations and caring leaders is conspicuous by its absence in educational research, policy, development, and practice. Given the centrality of formal school leaders in nurturing school culture, this creates highly problematic conditions for creating caring schools, a topic to which we return in the final section of the chapter.

What Does Care Look Like?

Over the last two decades, the concept of care has received increased attention. Our quest for knowledge has carried us through the disciplines (e.g., the organizational sciences, psychology), the professions (e.g., the ministry, nursing), and the philosophical sciences. In addition, understandings of care are threaded through other bodies of work. This is particularly true in the area of leadership where what we know comes from studies of servant, virtuous, authentic, and more leadership. So what have we learned about the texture of care?

To begin with, caring is marked by a series of "definitional dynamics." It is a mutual process in which someone (the carer) sees, identifies with, and responds in a competent manner to the needs of another (the cared for). Caring is an expression of values. Caring is shared. There is mutual engagement. It is not one way. It is a relational concept. It is grounded not on contracts or expected gains but on felt needs. It carries beyond feelings, however. Caring is action based. Caring is always context specific. It unfolds in real time in a certain setting. Caring is nonjudgmental in regards to persons. Actions can be labeled, people cannot. Caring attends to development and productive functioning, not to addressing deficits. And, as noted previously, caring is indirect. It touches the things that in turn promote personal growth and development.

In addition to the previously noted definitional dynamics, care can be unpacked into its "essential element"—in the same way that the academic program is defined by essential subjects (see Figure 12.1). Elements, in turn, are comprised of "factors." Specific "strategies," in turn, bring those factors to life. An illustration here is helpful. In Figure 12.2, we see that "membership" is one of the four essential elements of care. Three factors in turn combine to create the norm of membership: belonging, accomplishment, and recognition. Each of these factors becomes real through specific strategies or actions. If a school decides that working on the factor of "recognition" represents resources well invested, it would turn its attention to forming strategies to ensure that all students have meaningful opportunities to be acknowledged at school. A large number of possible strategies can be put into place to make acknowledgment a reality.

Figure 12.1 Caring Leadership: Overall Model

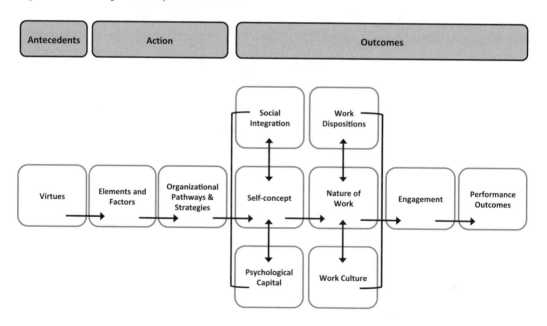

Figure 12.2 Caring Leadership: Antecedent and Action Phases

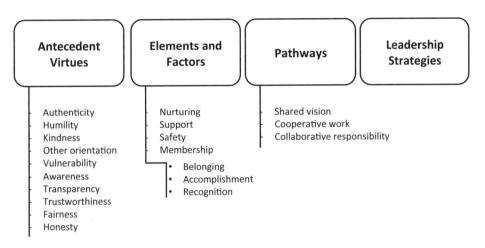

Also, Figure 12.1 illustrates the pathway by which caring leads to important outcomes. We see that caring nurtures the growth of three important conditions: integration into the school community, self-concept (e.g., self-esteem, self-efficacy, awareness, and so forth), and psychological capacity (e.g., motivation, hope, trust, resilience, and so forth). As caring relationships nurture these three conditions, three more distal outcomes blossom: work dispositions (e.g., mindfulness, commitment), nature of work (e.g., meaningfulness, creativeness), and work culture (e.g., community, cooperative work). This flow carries us to strengthened engagement, and because engagement is a direct proxy for performance, whether we are talking about children or teachers, learning is enhanced.

Caring Leaders

With the pillars of caring sketched out, we cycle back to the role of caring leaders. Random acts of caring are powerful events. But helping create a caring school is a more robust method of deepening caring and the just-discussed effects that caring promotes. And that opens the school leader door. We begin with an oft-forgotten reminder. To address the role of formal leaders in developing a caring school does not gainsay the need for or the value of dense understandings of leadership (i.e., shared, distributed, or collective leadership). It quite rightly reminds us, however, that formal leadership plays a pivotal role in determining whether a caring school materializes and flourishes. Formal leaders are a critical theme in the narrative of school improvement in general. They account for an important part of school success. In addition, we know that formal school leaders exert their primary influence on school culture, a reality that is becoming more pronounced as the academic side of the school improvement ledger becomes increasingly specified for schools. And remember that caring is about culture. Finally, we know that school leaders are even more critical in the culture of schools serving large numbers of students placed at peril by society and institutions. Without caring leaders, it is difficult to envision caring schools.

Caring leadership is essentially a moral orientation, the exercise of virtues formed and integrated across a lifetime in the service of others. While there is no universally accepted list that defines all virtuous leaders, theoretical and empirical work in the areas noted in the first section underscore virtues such as authenticity, humility, kindness, other focusedness (or service orientation), fairness, honesty, vulnerability, awareness, transparency, trustworthiness, and compassion as antecedents to caring leader practices. These antecedent virtues are quite different from those of more traditional power-oriented understandings of leadership. It is these virtues that provide "caring" to leader actions (e.g., that raise "cooperative work" from a method of completing assignments to a caring practice). Keeping in mind that it is the antecedent virtues that provide care to actions, we find that they often take form in acts of empowerment and enabling, acceptance, supportiveness, service, and forgiveness.

> We close with a restatement of four central themes. Care is the central pillar of school improvement. It is the taproot from which children are formed. And it is the purpose of schooling. We know that care is both an end and a means to valued outcomes for the cared for, caregivers, and the schools and communities in which the virtues of caring find a home, and we know that school leaders have an important role in determining if schools are transformed into communities of care.

Chapter 13

Principles for Developing Culturally Appropriate Schools

For over a half-century now we have sought ways to nurture the development of culturally relevant education. The best of this work begins with efforts to understand schooling through the eyes of children and their families—children of color, students from low-income and working-class homes, youngsters from various ethnicities and origins, young people with primary languages other than English, and so forth. Understanding in turn has helped fuel action. It has tempered singular reliance on ideological positioning to address the complexity and exhilaration of varied cultures in schools. More important, understanding has energized efforts to create authentic cultural responsiveness. History has proven to be an ally in this struggle. We see in our collective rearview mirror that much of the work here has often been weakly grounded in research. We see also that too routinely cultural relevance has meant adjusting children to a singular view of the world. These efforts have ranged from benign inattentiveness to promoting subtractive schooling.

In this chapter, I present what has been learned about effective and unproductive efforts to address diversity. We mold that knowledge into a design to create culturally responsive schools, one that features not sets of initiatives but rather an integrated and overlapping set of principles. I conclude that it is adherence to these principles that offers the promise of crafting authentic models of culturally appropriate schooling.

Principle of Affirmative Schooling

A considerable body of scholarship reveals that cultural marginalization is deeply woven into the tapestry of schooling. Schools are places where too often stereotypes determine actions, venues in which too often micro-aggressions go unseen, and if seen, unchallenged. In such schools, children are often allowed (expected) to exert minimal effort, to go through the motions of schooling, and to accept life on the sidelines. Thus, the first step in forging culturally appropriate schools is to nurture the principle of affirmative schooling. In these schools, youngsters are affirmed for who they are, not defined by what they lack (i.e., negatively). Educators in culturally appropriate schools do not pretend that students are unburdened by problems and challenges. However, they do not fall into the well-grooved pathway of "seeing" children through deficit eyes.

Principle of Justice

A second related principle is that adults and young people who struggle to create culturally appropriate places to learn and develop as people are sharply attentive to the concept of justice. This means, to begin with, that they have internalized school-grounded metrics of fairness and equity. They understand that these broad concepts must come to life in the normalcies and routines of everyday school life, in how students are addressed, in the expectations conveyed by language and actions, in the care and respect afforded to the less advantaged, and in how opportunities to learn are distributed. It also means that educators consciously create structures, policies, procedures, and activities to help justice go to root and flourish in schools. Equally important, it means that these tools are not simply organizational arrangements but that they are powered by a mixture of commitment and care.

Principle of Cultural Capital

Culturally responsive schools are dedicated to the principle that it is desirable to scaffold education on the cultural capital of students, families, and communities. We see here the threads of affirmation as well. Schools that are authentically involved with integrating community cultural capital are asset-based places. While they acknowledge the challenges that difference can surface, they are adept at pulling cultural capital into the work to ensure that each child reaches high levels of academic and social learning. These schools honor community norms and values in the quest for improvement. They do not ignore, silence, or disparage them. Such places understand at a deep level the essentiality of context in the quest to create productive schools for every child.

Principle of Care

As I have reported throughout this book, the principle of care is also at the heart of culturally responsive schools. In our work, we find that many children in culturally diverse schools are invisible or marginalized. They are tourists in their own schools, taking up space and doing just enough to get by. Our research tells us that while academic press is an essential aspect of care, classroom and school culture is even more important. Invisibility and marginalization are inconsistent with a climate of care. In tangible terms, the principle of care means that all children have meaningful, trusting relationships with their teachers. Each child is known as a student and as a person. Children are routinely recognized for their successes and for their contributions to the achievements of the school. Students have opportunities to be authentic members of the school community. They have stock ownership in the school. There are widespread opportunities for leadership throughout culturally responsive schools, and large numbers of children find themselves connected to those opportunities. Every child feels supported in school, that he is buttressed by teachers as well as peers. Finally, care in culturally appropriate schools is marked by a palpable ambience of safety and security.

Principle of Advocacy

In culturally appropriate schools, the principle of advocacy for children and their families is distinctly visible. Families in many of the schools that we spotlight herein (e.g., schools in immigrant neighborhoods) have noticeable disadvantages in navigating social institutions such as schools. That is, they have less knowledge about the rules of the game (e.g., how to access needed services). Consequently, their children are often placed in handicapped positions vis-à-vis opportunity. An essential element of culturally relevant schools is adults who act as powerful advocates for students who are not infrequently left behind, advocates for children in school and the larger community. Particularly salient here are teachers and school administrators who are adept at brokering support services and monitoring those services to ensure that diagnosed needs are being successfully addressed.

Principle of Instructional Relevance

Finally, we know that culturally appropriate schools are characterized by the principle of instructional relevance. Historically, this is the most emphasized component of culturally appropriate schooling. It is, of course, a critical element in the overall narrative. We place it last to remind ourselves that it is only one item in a package of big ideas that require attention to cultivate culturally relevant schools. On the instruction side of the educational program, we know that having teachers who look like the youngsters is important. So too is scaffolding instruction on platforms that are consistent with the cultures of the children in the school (e.g., cooperative learning for African American students). Using styles consistent with the cultures represented in the classroom is a wise strategy. On the curriculum side of the educational program, it is important for students to see themselves in the materials they encounter.

We know that building culturally appropriate schools is a powerful avenue to help many of our children who fail to reach their full potential. Here I argued based on research that the real work is less about interventions than it is about honoring core principles. As with almost everything in the world of school improvement, principles provide the seedbed in which strategies can grow. Also, it is the integration of the principles that makes success possible. No principle on its own can carry the day. Also, consistent with the larger school improvement agenda, it is the principles that provide authenticity to policies and structures, not the reverse.

In the larger narrative of school success, culturally relevant schools can make major differences in the lives of children. On one front, they help students learn more than peers in less fortunate schools. On an even larger front, they create hope and possibilities, qualities in short supply in many schools. They provide children with meaningful futures.

Chapter 14

The Other Wall: Communities of Pastoral Care for Students

(with Daniela Torre)

Over the last thirty-five years, researchers, developers, and school practitioners have substantially deepened our understanding of schools that work well for youngsters and their families. We have reported herein that schools that ensure that all students reach ambitious targets of performance are scaffolded on two foundational pillars that are braided together: strong academic press and supportive culture. Effective schooling is as simple and complex as this.

Based on this distilled knowledge and forensic analyses of schools' failures, a massive and vigorous assault on underachievement in America's schools has been engaged. New tools have been forged for the battle (e.g., charter schools, new standards). Older tools have been refurbished and polished anew (e.g., evaluation, accountability, time). At the center of this struggle has been a steadfast focus on making schools more academically challenging institutions and crafting strategies to help youngsters climb to levels of achievement that were considered unattainable for their parents and grandparents. This is wise policy and practice. As we have reported, strong academic press is a major component in the equation of school and student success. However, as we also reported, it is insufficient for many, perhaps the large majority of, young persons and for the overwhelming majority of students in peril of not reaching the new bar of success. What we know, but often fail to operationalize well, is that the culture that surrounds students and grows to define young people and their experiences in schools is critical in helping students rise to the demands of twenty-first-century schools. This is especially the case for those youngsters on whom we are rightfully bestowing new attention and action (i.e., students placed at risk).

The major difficulty with relying on the nearly exclusive focus on the academic side of school reform is that it ignores or pretends that the following foundational verities of education can be pushed aside.

- Students learn more from their peers than they do from adults.

- The "modal" level of student engagement is in the "passive disengagement" zone.

- Learning pivots first and foremost on relationships, not textbooks.

- Academic success often has to pass through the door of culture.

If we acknowledge and work from, not against, these realities, we arrive at the empirically anchored conclusion that schools need to add highly visible strands of support, what we previously labeled a culture of pastoral care, to the tapestry of school—not as an add-on or as a supplement to academics but as a foundational and integrated dimension of the educational enterprise. Many, perhaps most, children and adolescents are not going to be molded into better scholars using only an academic press.

In quite practical terms, this means that educators need to spend as much time and energy building, updating, and monitoring a "culture of pastoral care wall" as they do currently on the highly visible "academic achievement wall" found in most schools. In short, to help all students master ambitious learning targets, we need first to acknowledge the essential role of pastoral care in schools. Second, we need to be explicit about the components and elements that define a culture of care for students (e.g., membership). Third, because the tools to "assess" these components are rather primitive compared to those available to measure academic learning, we (practitioners, developers, and researchers) will need to spend the time required to forge and refine them. Fourth, we will need to be as religious in tabulating, displaying, and using this information to enrich pastoral care as we are in using data-driven decision making to nourish academic press. More accurately, we need to be much more expansive in how we conceptualize and define data-based decision making, creating a "wall" for supportive culture parallel to the one we have for academic press.

To set the stage for assignment three, we present our research-grounded insights about the components of pastoral care for students. Before we do so, however, we reinforce an essential plank in our analysis. While nurturing the development of pastoral care is productive and equitable in its own right, our concern here is upon its cardinal role in facilitating academic success. We report that the engine of pastoral care comprises four powerful norms: care, support, safety, and membership. Each of these norms, in turn, is made up of key ingredients, elements on which schools can track the positioning and growth of students and plan improvement strategies. For example, in Table 14.1 we outline the seven elements that define the norm of care. It is from here that the assessment of pastoral care can be plotted. As previously noted, however, unless we invest considerably more energy and resources on this half of the school success equation, a culture of pastoral care will remain a stepchild in the family of schooling.

Table 14.1   Elements of the Norm of Care

- Challenging students
- Making classes meaningful
- Emphasizing creative and active work
- Orchestrating structured classrooms
- Employing collaborative activities
- Pulling students to success
- Teaching beyond the textbook

The logic model also leads us to conclude that we need to be more aggressive, and more "scientific," about measuring the important conditions that mediate connections between the four norms and student learning. We think of these as intermediate outcomes: social integration, sense of self, and learning dispositions. A thick line of research tells us that the effects of a caring and supportive culture pass through these critical variables. We also know that, as was the case with the norms, each of these three states is comprised of essential elements. For example, the key ingredients of "sense of self" are listed in Table 14.2. And again, the elements provide the platform for needed assessments.

Table 14.2   Elements of Student Sense of Self

- Self-esteem
- Efficacy
- Resilience
- Agency
- Autonomy
- Identity
- Self-awareness

The research and model also reveal that these three intermediate outcomes exercise significant influence on student engagement, both student engagement with the school and, even more critically, student engagement with their schoolwork. Active, committed engagement, in turn, is the undisputed doorway to student social and academic learning.

> We know that a culture of pastoral care is critical to student learning. In this chapter, we portrayed this half of the school improvement algorithm and demonstrated how it works. Equally important, we presented our conclusion on the understudied state of pastoral care in schools and argued that good measures of the variables in the model are very much needed, much richer, and less ethereal assessments than we currently have at our disposal. We need to devote as much energy to displaying and using assessments of pastoral care to guide decision making in our schools as we do to academic press.

Chapter 15

Norms, Eyeballs, and Seedbeds

So where are we? We have covered a good deal of ground in these chapters. It is not my intention to review that work here. Suffice it to say that I attempted to create a portrait of the key elements of leadership and characteristics of school leaders. I attempted to do so in an integrated manner, to provide a center of gravity that holds all the aspects of leadership together. And I labored to make the knowledge practical, that is, of immediate use to school leaders.

The book is not a micro-level analysis of hundreds of specific actions that managers should perform. Neither is it a macro-level analysis of overarching constructs that defy operationalization. It provides, I argue, norms that ground the work of all effective school leaders. It is these mid-level concepts (e.g., demanding evidence for decisions, building organizations defined by shared responsibility) that determine powerful pathways to improvement. Without a framework of robust norms, leaders are likely to find themselves in the stratosphere or, equally unhelpful, wandering around in the weeds.

Another idea that cuts across the book is so obvious that I am hesitant to surface it explicitly. Specifically, leadership is a critical factor in the algorithm of quality schooling. It is very difficult to imagine a successful school that lacks effective leadership from those in formal management positions. It is nearly impossible to identify schools that have turned course from mediocre (or poor) to good absent the type of leadership we have seen in these chapters. So, leadership is important in general and even more critical for schools marooned in inlets of failure.

We also see that effective schools and their leaders are ferociously committed to two essential dynamics: creating instructional capacity and creating productive cultures for students, teachers, and parents or caregivers. The work of successful leaders is as simple and complex as this. It is simple in the sense that what needs to be done is neither unknown nor hidden. The path forward is actually quite clear. It is complex in the sense that pursuing the path is arduous and demanding. People will naturally suggest following less strenuous paths. They are apt to turn back when barriers are uncovered. Energy is hardly an unlimited resource.

So leadership is critical. Leaders need one eyeball consistently focused on academic press and the other on productive culture. And the best leaders operate not from binders and notebooks or abstract tenets but powerful norms (such as support, collaborative work, and evidence-based decision making) that inform and direct practices and behaviors. Our work in these chapters conveys one additional lesson. Great leaders are caretakers of organizational seedbeds. They know intuitively and from hard-forged experiences that planting school reforms in toxic soil ensures that improvements will never take root and flourish. They understand that it is unhelpful to drag a succession of very-likely-to-fail initiatives into their schools. Their task is to haul away bureaucratic organizational and behaviorist learning soil and build seedbeds of community and constructivism. It is only at this point that student-centered and developmentally focused changes can be productive.

References

Ancess, J. (2003). *Beating the odds: High schools as communities of commitment.* New York: Teachers College Press.

Bauman, P. C. (1996). Governing education in an antigovernment environment. *Journal of School Leadership, 6*(6), 625–643.

Bolman, L. G., & Deal, T. E. (2011). *Leading with soul: An uncommon journey of spirit.* Hoboken, NJ: John Wiley & Sons.

Bryk, A. S., Sebring, P. B., & Allensworth, E. (2010). *Organizing schools for improvement: Lessons from Chicago.* Chicago: University of Chicago.

Crosnoe, R. (2011). *Fitting in, standing out: Navigating the social challenges of high school to get an education.* Cambridge: Cambridge University Press.

Csikszentmihalyi, M., & Larson, R. (1984). *Being adolescent: Conflict and growth in the teenage years.* New York: Basic Books.

Dahrendorf, R. (1995). A precarious balance. Economic opportunity, civil society, and political liberty. *The Responsive Community,* 13–39.

Elmore, R. F. (1995). Structural reform and educational practice. *Educational Researcher, 24*(9), 23–26.

Hattie, J. A. C. (2009). *Visible learning: A synthesis of over 900 meta-analyses relating to achievement.* London: Routledge.

Himmelstein, J. L. (1983). The new right. In R. C. Liebman & R. Wuthnow (Eds.). *The new Christian right: Mobilization and legitimization* (pp. 13–30). New York: Aldine.

Interstate School Leaders Consortium. (1996). *Standards for school leaders.* Washington, DC: Council of Chief State School Officers.

Kirst, M. & Meister, G. (1985). Turbulence in American secondary schools: What reforms last? *Curriculum Inquiry, 15*(2), 169–186.

Murphy, J. (2000, February). Governing America's schools: The shifting playing field. *Teachers College Record, 102*(1), 57–84.

Rauner, D. M. (2000). *They still pick me up when I fall: The role of caring in youth develop-ment and community life.* New York: Columbia University Press.

Tomlinson, J. (1986). Public education, public good. *Oxford Review of Education, 12*(3), 211–222.

Tushman, M. L., & Romanelli, E. (1985). Organizational evolution: A metamorphosis model of convergence and reorientation. In L. L. Cummings & B. M. Straw (Eds.), *Research in organizational behavior* (pp. 171–222). Greenwich, CT: JAI Press.

Tyack, D. (1993). School governance in the United States: Historical puzzles and anoma-lies. In J. Hannaway & M. Carnoy (Eds.), *Decentralization and school improvement* (pp. 1–32). San Francisco: Jossey-Bass.

Yair, G. (2000). Not just about time: Instructional practices and productive time in school. *Educational Administration Quarterly, 36*(4), 485–512.

Index